KU-175-867

add some music to your day

Analyzing and Enjoying the Music of the Beach Boys

Edited by

Don Cunningham and Jeff Bleiel

Tiny Ripple Books
P.O. Box 1533
Cranberry Township, PA 16066

Published by:
Tiny Ripple Books
P.O. Box 1533
Cranberry Township, PA 16066
www.tinyripple.com

Copyright © 2000 Jeff Bleiel and Don Cunningham
All rights reserved including the right of reproduction in whole or in part in any form.
ISBN 0-9675973-0-7
Library of Congress Catalog Card Number: 99-68551
Printed in the United States of America
Cover photo: 1979 Caribou Records publicity photo

For Natalie, Laura, Vicki, and Nicky

contents

preface

Ah, writings from one's youth. When the heart was loud and pumping fast. Complexities of language were undiscovered, and typos and misspellings amounted to a theme. I was inexperienced, with less to lose, and enraptured by the artistry in a musical canon. Today finds me middle-aged, a comfortably settled gentleman typically enjoying a pinch of brandy and listening to Lauritz Melchior on the player—and occasionally emerging from the manor to fight crime in the metropolis (but I've said too much).

You are holding a book of essays first published in the fan journal *Add Some Music*. In 1978, still flush with enthusiasm for the reemergence in public and on vinyl of Brian Wilson ("Brian Is Back," 1976), I created a forum in which Wilson's music and the activities of his band, the Beach Boys, were discussed in depth. I was encouraged by another journal, *Pet Sounds*, which writer David Leaf had published. I modeled mine on the digest-sized *Dickens Quarterly*. Sixteen issues of *Add Some Music* were mailed to dedicated subscribers worldwide from late 1978 to mid 1984.

The journal offered more than what is here. For this book, editor Jeff Bleiel and I have chosen only those essays that seemed to have lasting value and offered analysis and perhaps revelation. Other pieces—discographies, news items, and more—pulled in other directions and supported our purpose less well. We also have included two pieces that did not appear in the journal: "A Children's Song," which I wrote for *Endless Summer Quarterly* in 1994, and "Their Hearts Were Full Of Spring," which Jeff wrote in 1999.

We have edited the essays. This is not a reproduction of an artifact. We strove to maintain the flavor and content of each original piece and added no new information other than a few explanatory notes. But we corrected misspellings, replaced wrong words, and followed rules of grammar. Our goal was to produce a book that would flow and inform while staying close to the original spirit of *Add Some Music*.

My thanks go to the writers whose essays are reprinted in this book and to others who contributed in valuable ways: Andrew Bainborough, Mike Clark, Lee Dempsey, Tim Earnshaw, Brad Elliott, John Galvin, Brian Gari, Francis Greene, Gerhard Honekamp, David Leaf, Jim Lucerino, Stephen Peters, Peter Reum, Greg Szyszkowski, and many many more. I especially thank Brian Berry, who provided so many terrific photographs for the issues (many of which are reproduced here), and Jeff Bleiel, one of those blessed original subscribers, who now has produced this book.

Don Cunningham
September 1999

preface

Editing and organizing the articles that comprise this book has confirmed my initial belief that Don Cunningham's journal *Add Some Music* contained some truly original and insightful commentary on the art of that great American institution, The Beach Boys. The quality and insight of the writing exceeded its then-limited distribution, and although there is no shortage of available literature on the Beach Boys nowadays, these pieces stand up as worthy of reintroduction to the public.

I was in the beginning phases of my infatuation with the group when I answered a 1979 *Rolling Stone* ad which promised a "serious publication dedicated to the music of the Beach Boys." Those quarterly issues of *Add Some Music* provided me with welcome news on the band's activities (much harder to come by in those pre-Internet days), and a sense of belonging to a community involved in thoughtful, occasionally eloquent, communication about the fact that this art ran deeper than ditties about surfing.

For me, digging back into the pages of *Add Some Music* has been, in some ways, akin to fondly recalling the naivete of a youthful love affair. It is quite intentional that this book does not present a 1999 perspective of the Beach Boys. There is praise for songs that may not have stood the test of time. Importance is placed on events that may now seem unimportant. There is hope that has proven to be unrealized. We now know so much more about the Beach Boys as men, as artists, as litigants, as survivors, as succumbers. We've now heard material that was then locked in the vaults. But it is important to read these essays from the place where their writers' (and readers') hearts were in the late '70s and early '80s. The feelings of that era were very valid, and should not be lost or forgotten in Beach Boys history.

I'd like to thank Don Cunningham for the effort and faith he's invested in this project. Thanks also to Nicky Bleiel, Ann Moats, Robbie Leff, and Michael White.

Jeff Bleiel
September 1999

help me, rhonda

By Don Cunningham

(Originally published in February 1982)

It was March 1965. More than 4 months had passed since the release of a new Beach Boys album, and Capitol big shots were naturally getting nervous. They knew that Brian Wilson was hard at work on new material, but could they continue to bank on this kid? Could Wilson follow up on the smashes of the previous year—"Fun, Fun, Fun," "Little Honda," "I Get Around," "Don't Worry Baby," "Dance, Dance, Dance?" At least that last song about dancing would be on the new album. And there would be another song about dancing. That seemed promising.

In March *The Beach Boys Today!* was released. It took a month to get to the top ten, then stayed there for 14 weeks. "Do You Wanna Dance," the other "dance" song, charted respectably as the single, just missing the top ten. That's OK, thought the Capitol thinkers, one finds better profits in album sales. Kids were slow-dancing to "Kiss Me Baby," and everything was copacetic.

As the Capitol big shots were scrutinizing their bottom lines in 1965, other persons were taking note of another occurrence: the developing artistry of Brian Wilson. As soon as *Today* was released, another artist, Johnny Rivers, expressed an interest in covering one of Wilson's new songs on the album. The song was "Help Me, Rhonda," and Brian knew better than to let it slip through his fingers. He saw the song's potential as an AM radio hit, returned to the studio to recut it, and released it as the next Beach Boys' single.

Bang! "Help Me, Rhonda" becomes the number one song in the United States. Brian Wilson follows his 1964 successes with a rousing rocker with a strange personal title, and the country loves it. Seventeen years later, are any breathing inhabitants of this land unfamiliar with the refrain, "Help me Rhonda, help, help me Rhonda"?

1

With "Help Me, Rhonda" Wilson did more than produce a new hit. He showed that he could reach new plateaus and that he could create new plateaus. Needless to say, he was far from finished. The seriousness with which this man was approaching the modern popular music scene was only beginning to be noticed, and the extent of his influence was still modest. "Help Me, Rhonda" would be the most obvious manifestation of Brian Wilson as an American folk artist, although it would not be the best example of the range of qualities that would eventually distinguish his work.

A discussion of "Help Me, Rhonda" must mention two distinctly different versions. The original *Today* album version and subsequent single version differ as night and day, with each emphasizing one of the dual concerns of Wilson: art and commerciality. I am partial to the original version because of its richer, more delicate textures, yet I listen in awe to the power emanating from Brian's brash revision for single release.

With its firm, fast, drum-defined rhythms, "Help Me, Rhonda" should be classified as a rocker. Yet, among the fast songs of Brian's early years, it stands apart because of its length — more than 3 minutes in its initial form (his early fast songs were 2 to 2.5 minutes in length). As opposed to the slam-bam-thank-you-ma'am nature of "I Get Around," "Fun, Fun, Fun," and "Dance, Dance, Dance," Wilson's new rocker was more drawn out, more R&B flavored, rooted more in the songwriting school of Spector, crossing over from pure pop to a mixture of rhythmic influences.

> **Are any breathing inhabitants of this land unfamiliar with the refrain "Help me Rhonda, help, help me Rhonda?"**

"Help Me, Rhonda" likely was considered a modest album cut, with its easy lyricism, laid-back R&B rhythm, and longer form. Capitol contributed its own opinion about the song's worth by misspelling "Ronda" on the *Today* album jacket. Few persons initially noticed that "Help Me, Rhonda" could grasp the listener immediately—and then permanently. Yet it could and it did and it does.

The album version begins with a counterpoint of two irresistible and memorable themes: the syncopated downward-spiraling guitar theme and the bouncing bass figure. In the single version, Brian improved on the

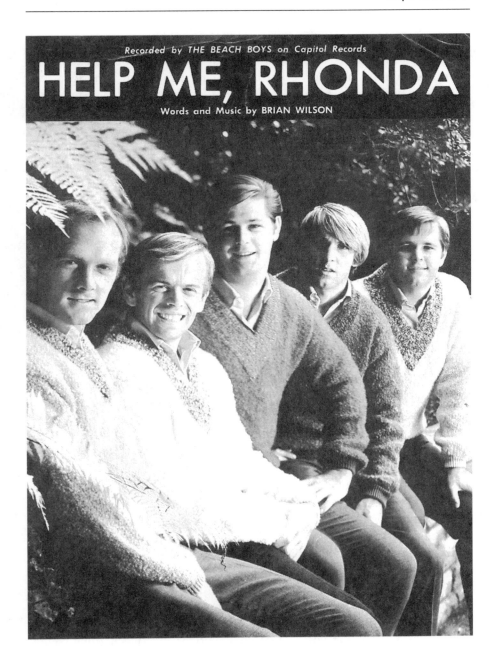

bass part, making it a circular motion, an inversion of the guitar riff. The drum leaps in with its incessant biological beat, your body picks up the beat, and you are hooked. Next comes Al Jardine's all-American lead vocal — icing on the cake.

The crucially familiar I-IV-I harmonic cadence underscores a verse melody of inspired genius. The twists and turns and internal rhythms could only be created by Wilson. Jardine sings "Well since she put me down..." in a manner that evidences the wishes of Wilson while delivering its own populist values. Jardine interprets the mock pain in the lyric with good-hearted sincerity, making "Help Me, Rhonda" a song about fun and hope. Like all great melodies, that of "Help Me, Rhonda" is both simple and inspired. It is a good friend.

The album version continues a standard key development, with guitar, tambourine, and bass providing exciting texture under Jardine's vocal. Then, in a song filled with sublime hooks, we reach the hook of hooks— the bridge into the chorus: "Bom, bom, bom, bom, bom, bom, bom..." The first version does not vocalize this bridge, although anyone who has heard the latter version will be unable to resist providing a vocalization. This chant resembles the early guitar theme but is more singable. When performed in concert, "Help Me, Rhonda" is always the final straw, breaking the most die hard nonsingers into song — while throwing every last body into the mass dance.

And that is because it is a song to be danced to. In the *Today* version, after moving through another verse and chorus, Wilson shifts into an instrumental "middle," dominated by the throbbing bass, tambourine, and guitar. My feeling is that he has the dance in mind. The chorus reappears and repeats, fading in and out dynamically in a surprising manner which is not altogether successful. Again, I believe he has the dance in mind.

For my money, the most precious moments in "Help Me, Rhonda" occur when the boys sing two words: "fine" and "eye." Here are cases of that complex harmonic "drift" that characterizes the Beach Boys sound. It is a signature, the combination of Brian's vocal arrangement and the blood-related voices. Unique, priceless.

Turning attention to Wilson's revision of "Help Me, Rhonda" for single release, we should first notice the transparency of his attempt to create an AM radio hit. It is obvious in the way Alan's voice is pushed up in the mix so that he comes crackling out of the speaker. It is evident in Brian's further development of hooks: the cyclic bass theme; the "bom bom boms"; the new "come on Rhonda," which, in concert, has become a strong theme. The clincher is the tremendous electric guitar riff added to the instrumental break. And the break itself is telescoped.

In the effort to appeal through the AM radio speaker, the second version loses the inspired textures of Brian's original production. The tambourine gets lost under the louder guitars and Jardine's dominant vocal. The R&B feel in the original yields to a more jumping rock style. Even the manner in which "eye" and "fine" are sung is changed.

Wilson has stated his debt to Buster Brown's "Fanny Mae" for the harmonica hook used during the break of "Help Me, Rhonda." Another reference, which, as far as I know, has not been made, is the influence of "Then He Kissed Me," the Spector/Crystals hit of 1963. Like Spector's track, Brian placed "Help Me, Rhonda" (as well as Brian's own version of "Then He Kissed Me" for the *Summer Days* album) in the key of D-flat. This decision likely

> The most precious moments in "Help Me, Rhonda" occur when the boys sing two words: fine and eye.

was made as well out of deference to Jardine's vocal ability (the *Summer Days* song also features Jardine on lead vocal). A great similarity exists between the rhythms and harmonic plots of the main verses in both songs. Sing "Well since she put me down..." and then sing "Well I walked up to her..." Differences appear soon after the verses, but a connection can be made.

Any songwriter will tell you there is nothing wrong with reusing an old hook. This may even be construed as a tribute, especially when an old theme is fit into a new environment to the mutual benefit of both. The fact is, all melodic phrases have been incorporated into songs. It is now a matter of dressing them up differently.

For a song to be a folk song, it must fulfill certain requirements. Of all the qualities that can be associated with folk songs, from a consciousness of the average man to the repetitive and lyrical nature of a melody, one virtue stands out: a folk song simply endures. Brian Wilson's song about "gittin' her outta my heart," contains most of the qualities of a folk song. As Alan Jardine sings of "out doin' in my head," and we are not sure just what he is talking about, a fact remains: "Help Me, Rhonda" remains. It will continue to endure.

yesterday and today

By Don Cunningham

(Originally published in December 1980)

On December 31, 1961, the Beach Boys performed three songs at the Ritchie Valens memorial rock and roll show. A bunch of kids still wet behind the ears, they drew a positive response for their first semi-hit, "Surfin'." It was light and spirited rock and roll. Because of the vocal stylings, especially supported by Mike Love, the sound was new, even if it didn't herald an enormous event.

In England at that time, another new sound was heard, this one having to do with the voices of John Lennon and Paul McCartney and the guitars of Lennon and George Harrison. This sound did herald an enormous event.

Both sounds were conceived in the American rock and roll womb of the 1950s. Both gestated in the hearts of lower-middle-class boys.

By the mid-Sixties, the Beatles' sound constituted a sustained explosion so immense that it helped change a cultural/social consciousness. As it turned out (and was recognized then), the genius of Lennon and McCartney lay in their ability to fashion lyrics and music that worked together to shift musical and cultural currents.

Brian Wilson's music did not explode. He worked within the currents of the times, or so it seemed. Because his lyrics had less perception than his music, we had the impression, as stated in those lyrics, that Brian was following, not leading. A genius lay hidden to some extent—but not to the Beatles, who heard the things Brian was doing and were affected by them. And by the 1970s, it had become evident that, on a grand scale, something just as important musically had been occurring within the grooves of all those orange-labeled singles that bore the imprint "The Beach Boys."

7

Today in 1980, two decades after the Beach Boys' beginning, their music sits curiously alongside the music of the Beatles. The Beatles did not continue to affect the culture strongly after their explosion. There was some catching up to do, but the music of Brian Wilson and the Beach Boys is now recognized as a cultural phenomenon ranking with that of the Beatles.

repairing the arid landscape

the surf's up album ♩ ♩♪

By Michael Bocchini

(Originally published in September 1980)

In 1971, the Beach Boys released their second album for Warner/ Reprise, *Surf's Up*. Conditions could not have appeared worse. Brian remained in his self-imposed exile, and Dennis, whose work had shown great promise on *Sunflower*, had injured his hand in an accidental confrontation with a glass door. But working under the amorphous production credit of "The Beach Boys," the group completed a surprisingly unified and satisfying work.

The original release of *Surf's Up* included an insert which contained the album's lyrics backed by a brown-tint photograph of an arid landscape. This insert marked the first time that lyrics accompanied a Beach Boys' album, and the first time the group attempted to involve the listener visually with the thematic content of an LP.

The insert photograph and the LP's opening track, "Don't Go Near The Water," borrow from the epic convention of beginning a story in the middle rather than the start. In every measure of life – social, ecological, artistic, psychological – the decade of the 1960s had forced man to confront the abuses of the past. The vision of an arid landscape whose texture had been cracked apart, combined with the sound of the plaintive voices of Beach Boys singing of the corruption of the water, summarize an era of ecological, social, and self-abuse.

The album rejects the fixed image of a never-ending wasteland, however. In beautifully realized integration, *Surf's Up* calls its listener to action. The rejection of the working title *Landlocked* emerges as a thematic choice, not

9

just a note of homage to Brian's contribution from *Smile*. While land-locked despair characterizes the album's starting point, hope waits at the end of the *Surf's Up* musical quest.

Repairing the cracked fabric of a worldview does not come easily. Each working member of the group confronts the task in a highly personalized manner, which results in a unified mosaic of understandably human responses. Carl collaborated with Jack Rieley on "Long Promised Road" and "Feel Flows" to produce a mystical and metaphorical response. Al Jardine collaborated with Gary Winfrey to produce a clear and craftsmanlike everyman response. Bruce Johnston contributed "Disney Girls (1957)" with its lush, nostalgic response, and Mike Love contributed "Student Demonstration Time," which counsels retreat.

> **Perhaps no other rock album of the 1970s addresses itself so thoroughly to the challenges of modern societies.**

Brian Wilson's three contributions serve as a reprise of the album's movement through problem, despair and hope. Ironically, the self-exiled member, least able to cope with existent reality, contributes the cement that binds when he reaches back to 1966 and "Surf's Up."

"Long Promised Road" is composed with an AB-AB-C-AB-BB structure. Each A movement begins with Carl's soft voice and an even softer harmony. In this mood, the song speaks of the difficulty of the human spirit in rising above images of pain ("So hard to laugh a child-like giggle when the tears start to torture my mind").

However, Carl's voice, the harmonies, and the instrumentation rise to a harder rock sound as they slip into the B sections to "hit hard at the battle that's confronting" them.

The point/counterpoint continues until the C movement. At the center of the pain and struggle rests the long promised road. Here, Carl's voice is gentle and reassuring as the harmonies and rippling organ promise tranquility at the end of a struggle to liberate a person from the "pain of growing in soul" and "climbing up to reality's goal." The problems remain, hence the final A. But the struggle is joined with renewed vigor as the song ends with three consecutive (and consecutively stronger) B movements.

With "Feel Flows," any point/counterpoint stridency has been removed. Every production element radiates tranquility and harmony. The images of suffering (clouds, wind) remain and threatening questions still confront. However, they fade in significance when one can "Feel Flows."

Carl's voice contains no yea/nay emotions as he sings of consolation and strife. Alliteration and rhyme blend them into a oneness as the instrumentation undulates and the harmony unifies. The song speaks of a divinity which lies within and without all things and directs all events. To be in touch with this flow is to liberate through surrender.

During the song's instrumental break, the past dominates in the Renaissance flavor of Charles Lloyd's airy flute. The present is fittingly brief in the form of a short piano riff. The no longer fearful future, in the form of a synthesizer, joins the flute and piano as the now familiar undulating chords continue throughout the break and into the song's resolution. All man sees as separate is one: feel flows.

With the richness and profundity of Carl's contribution to the album's concept, one might overlook the solid nature of Al Jardine's efforts. His metaphors may not be as complex, but their meanings are necessary to appreciate the whole. The problems of the arid world touch every man, not just the philosopher.

"Take A Load Off Your Feet" may borrow its car horns and assorted banging pipe sounds from the Spike Jones school of musical effects, yet its thematic intent is dead but not deadly serious. Getting lost in those twinkled, wrinkled toes leaves one unmindful of the "piece of glass" and "treacherous blows." The cutting refrain, "Better take care of your life 'cause nobody else will," is not devoid of social criticism and cynical advice on the part of a person who has seen more than his share of world hurt.

"Lookin' At Tomorrow (A Welfare Song)" follows "Feel Flows" and serves as a fine companion piece. The song treats darkness and light, disappointment and fulfillment, and work and repose with the evenhandedness

11

of "Feel Flows," but with Al's characteristic simplicity and clarity. No divinity shapes this serenity. The love of a man and a woman replenishes man and assuages the harshness of modern existence.

Bruce Johnston's "Disney Girls (1957)," like "Lookin' At Tomorrow," offers love as a solution. But Johnston's is not love that must face hardship: "Reality, it's not for me and it makes me laugh," he sings. "But fantasy world and Disney girls, I'm coming back." The escapist world of TV and a nostalgic past which never existed is offered as a hollow solution. Rick and Dave and Pop's ice cream would quickly melt on the landscape pictured on the album's insert.

12

This dream is as soft and beautiful as Johnston's song and as fragile as Johnston's voice. The song's production displays the lush richness of the Beach Boys at their harmonic best. As the song fades with its soft whistling one is tempted to join this beautiful escapism and forget the reality which surrounds this fragile balance.

"Student Demonstration Time" allows no such escape. The world is a cell block and humanity the prisoners. Horns blare, sirens wail, a piano throbs, and guitars blast to crush Johnston's airy bubble. Mike Love catalogs the trauma of the recent past (Berkeley, Jackson State, Kent State) to thrust the picture insert into the listener's view once more. Rick and Dave and Pop must give way to TV's new world of violence, com-

> With the richness and profundity of Carl's contribution to the album's concept, one might overlook the solid nature of Al Jardine's efforts.

pletely unrehearsed, on the evening news. The positioning of these songs at the close of side one enhances the value of "Feel Flows" at the top of the second side.

Brian Wilson's contribution to *Surf's Up* constitutes a trilogy of reprise. The condition of the ecology is personified in the voice of a dying tree in "A Day In The Life Of A Tree." Jack Rieley's lead vocal is raspy and broken, yet his lyric speaks poignantly of the interdependence of man and nature. The harming of nature is characterized as an act of self-abuse – "now my branches suffer and my leaves don't offer poetry to men of song."

The funereal sound of the organ interjects a strong note of despair into the song. Without the inspiration of nature, man finds himself without the patterns of eternal rhythms from which he can fashion the songs to uplift his spirit.

Man is left without the connections necessary for an integrated life. "'Til I Die" extends this thought through a series of metaphors for this feeling of helplessness. The organ is reintroduced, but its ponderous feeling is lacking. A series of chord progressions produces the effect of an airy, slow-motion movement, threatening and reassuring at the same time.

13

The song projects a sense of human abandonment to the forces of nature without the needed understanding of their immutable patterns. The lyric projects none of the reassurance found in the instrumentation. The tree can welcome death as an end to the ravages of mankind, for death constitutes a part of the natural cycle. But a man adrift must fear this solution. To him, death's release is only the terrifying thought of an end to existence. And his mind reverberates with this thought in contrapuntal force — "These things I'll be until I die." These two songs describe the natural and psychological wasteland produced by modern man.

In "Surf's Up," the themes of the album crystallize. The fact that a 1966 song speaks so eloquently to the album's topicality illustrates the timelessness of these problems and their solutions.

"Surf's Up" must be recognized as a composition of incredible richness. The song reflects awareness as the surf reflects the early morning sun. Van Dyke Parks' lyric shimmers with literary and biographical allusions as the music shifts between simplicity and complexity. Voices join and separate as they rise and fall through harmony and counterpoint.

Like many of the major fragments of the *Smile* album, "Surf's Up" displays a concern for the American experience and its contradictions. The song's first stanza moves the American saga from Queen Isabella's opening gambit ("A diamond necklace played the pawn") through colonization ("hand in hand some drummed along") and the blind march of expansion ("to a handsome man and baton") on to the period of self examination as in the distorted but perceptive vision of Edgar Allan Poe ("Back through the opera glass you see the pit and the pendulum drawn."). Poe spoke of the dark underside of America, and his observations caused many in the nation to reexamine their most closely held values, to find them lacking ("columnated ruins domino"), and to call for a reworking of priorities. But the calls fell on deaf ears ("canvass the town and brush the backdrop / Are you sleeping?").

> A simple piano, the lone instrumentation, rises from below, a "cellar tune" to guide these movements.

14

The second stanza belongs to the autobiographical persona of Brian Wilson. A child of the American dream whose songs evoked the fullness of the American myth, Brian's persona is the voice of a man broken by success. His music has dissolved in the awareness that the price paid has been too high.

The trumpet which triumphantly sounded the beginning of "Surf's Up" has become a muted "trumpeter's swan" song of taps, and the xylophone which underscored the allusion to Poe's grim insight and unheeded call sounds again. For failing to understand the message of Poe (a favorite author of young Brian Wilson), Brian has been forced to live the metaphor and painfully reach awareness which shatters personal belief. The call for change is refrained with the hope that it will be embraced by the listener.

From this point, "Surf's Up" is dominated by combined opposites. The lyric takes on a complexity of diction and image. Muted lights dimly illuminate the darkness and fog. Yet one must cast off ("at port adieu or die"). No false bravado of "Don't Back Down" here. These are the movements of a broken man who steels himself for a desperate attempt at redemption.

However, throughout this lyric of stress, a simple piano, the lone instrumentation, rises from below, a "cellar tune" to guide these movements. This evenhanded instrumentation links "Surf's Up" with the undulating instrumentation of "Feel Flows" and the eternal cycles of nature.

The piano continues as voices strike a note of renewed hope – surf's up. The direction of humanity's and America's future must be changed ("come about hard").

The solutions rest with man's earliest encounters with his environment. In the rhythms of spring, renewal can be found. In a children's song, redemption can be found. The remembered simplicity of nature's renewal and the simple beauty of a child's song of love connect man with the faith to restore the landscape and his psyche.

In the middle of the 1800s William Wordsworth faced the ravages of the Industrial Revolution and his poetry spoke of the dangers of man's reckless pursuit of profit and progress. In the introduction to his now-famous poem, "Ode: Intimations Of Immortality," he writes, "The child is father of the man."

Wordsworth's ode also mentions a tree which speaks of "something missing." The inspiration of the Van Dyke Parks/Brian Wilson collaboration is not in doubt.

As "Surf's Up" (both the song and the album) reaches a conclusion, voices meet in counterpoint as though the various voices of enlightenment throughout the ages come forth with their consistent message of hope and direction — "The child is the father of the man."

Perhaps no other rock album of the 1970s addresses itself so thoroughly to the challenge of modern societies. The disparate personalities and talents of the Beach Boys coalesced to produce an album of harmonious insight and musical accomplishment and an album whose message and art remain largely unheeded and unheralded.

god only knows

By Don Cunningham

(Originally published in February 1983)

Over the years, the task of minding the store of Brian Wilson music has fallen to the other Beach Boys, and their planning and execution has left much to be desired. A modus operandi has developed including cryptic plans, false starts, missed chances, and just plain bad ideas.

Yet despite the famous difficulties, there have been real successes. Although Brian's intractable nature has thrown the working band into career tailspins, at times his innate talents and strong art have risen to the fore and given the band a desperately needed shot in the arm. The Beach Boy machine springs back to life, again and again, because of Brian. So it has been with "Surf's Up," "Sail On Sailor," "Marcella," "Rock And Roll Music," *Love You*, sold-out concerts, HBO videos, and Sunkist commercials.

Then there are the ideas smaller in scope but successful for the same basic reason (Brian's art). I am thinking in particular of the playing of the London Symphony Orchestra's version of "God Only Knows" in auditoriums prior to performances. For a couple of years now, in the break between opening act and live Beach Boys, concert-goers have been treated to this sensitive, slowed-down instrumental recording of Brian Wilson's major opus.

What a marvelous idea. Could any Beach Boy have calculated the impact, on so many levels, of this offering? Might any planner for the group have predicted that the song would affect the listener in such a profound way? While sitting back and waiting for the Beach Boys to appear, one is usually struck by thoughts of a perspective nature. This great and good American band, this artistic institution, is once again about to perform—right now, for the nth time. Thoughts turn to the curious course of the band's history, to the meaning of the music and its success, to the enigma that is Brian Wilson.

19

Indeed the minutes leading to the Beach Boys' entrance should be used for such meditation. And as if someone understood that fact, the music of "God Only Knows" makes its way through the crowd, not only providing an apt aural environment for such contemplation, but also serving as an active catalyst to bring deep thoughts to the surface. With its warm and drawn-out presentation of the special chords Wilson worked into "God Only Knows," the London Orchestra's rendition stretches one's mind back to the days of 1966 and the musical and psychological setting that produced the song.

It is a study of the song, of the group, of the artist Brian Wilson. As the orchestra allows each chord to unfold, the listener mentally fills in the time/space with combined feelings of gentle euphoria and sadness. An artist has been at work, and we think back to the days of great labor and boisterous success. For those in the right frame of mind, this orchestral version of "God Only Knows" will conjure the soul of Brian Wilson before the Beach Boys launch into their first song of the night.

Of course when Wilson set out to write and produce "God Only Knows" in 1966, there were no such analytical thoughts. They were the days of the real thing, when a kind of electric creativity dominated recording sessions, when Brian's songwriting and productions were benefiting from a culmination of his abilities. Forces were coming together in a providential timetable. Brian could use the energy derived from the successful days of '63, '64, and '65 and combine it with fully matured ideas about record-making to create masterpieces. He could take brilliant, original ideas about tonality and temper them with his instinctual understanding, from boyhood days, of the traditional melodic structures of American pop-folk song. In so doing, he would produce melodies for a new folk classicism.

Considering that Paul McCartney is the most successful songwriter of all time, one should not take lightly McCartney's statement proclaiming "God Only Knows" the greatest pop song ever. I would venture that even he encountered difficulty in attempting to find the tonal center in the song.

However, a tonal center exists, as "God Only Knows" consists of a beautifully inventive plot within the key of E-major. The eight instrumental measures that begin the song are simple IV-I cadences, which show up again in the chorus ("And God only knows...") and then again in the tag-ending. The bass figures beneath those chords are something else, however—something pure Brian Wilson. The bass descends slowly, an interval at a time. It is the root of the opening A chord; then the third of the tonic E chord; then the sixth of the next A chord (or root of F-sharp); and finally the root of the tonic E, yielding a resolution of sorts.

The plucked syncopated half notes of the bass as it descends in this introduction appeal to the senses in two ways. In tonal relation to each other, they provide color and character—the slow, careful descent. In tonal relation to the chords above, they create both resolution (usually as root notes) and counter relationships (thirds, etc.). In this way the bass contributes to the overall plot in more ways than you might expect.

That was perhaps too technical, yet the inspired tonal concepts in the verses demand even more technical appreciation. Keeping it simple, notice how a bass figure acts as a bridge into the first verse, and that, oddly enough, the verse begins with a D chord (the tone leading to E, as opposed to E). The plot thickens with regard to chords presented and the underlying bass. There is a subtle battle between the keys of D and E, with E eventually winning out. Surely the tonal movements in the verse of "God Only Knows" were unexpected in 1966; today they remain adventurous. Knowledge that these tonal constructions are so removed from the commonplace adds to the beauty of the song, and makes Paul McCartney say things of a superlative nature.

> Surely the tonal movements in the verse of "God Only Knows" were unexpected in 1966; today they remain adventurous.

Artists come to be known by their harmonies, by the key systems they usually employ, by certain tonal progressions they prefer. Such considerations provide the listener with a sort of personality profile of the songwriter and distinguish a George Gershwin from a Cole Porter, a Brian Wilson from a Paul McCartney. More obvious than those harmonic traits are the rhythmic proclivities of the artists and less obvious are the subtle formations of melody.

Like the most deeply hidden aspects of the artist's personality, the nuances of melody are so slight as to be unrevealed as parts. In the whole, however, a Brian Wilson melody can be observed and distinguished from a McCartney melody or a Paul Simon melody. When I attempt to compare Wilson's melody in "God Only Knows" to others, I keep coming up with Stephen Foster.

Moreover, the "God Only Knows" melody is based on a triplet theme containing a half-tone interval. Witness "I may not," "long as there," "you nev-er," "make you so," and "God on-ly." This theme is presented on various tonal levels as the melody gently rises and falls and rises and falls. Other three-note figures abound ("above you," "to doubt it") and, all told, there is a meaningful relationship between these melodic-rhythmic figures and the syncopated half-notes in the bass.

The lyricism of "God Only Knows" reminds me of Foster's "Jeanie with the Light Brown Hair" with regard to the melodic three-note themes and the gentle, classical movement of notes up and down. Furthermore, a small case can be made by comparing the way in which both writers fuse rhythm and lyricism into melody.

So much for surfing down the Swanee River. A discussion of the rhythm track in "God Only Knows" requires a shifting in historical perspective to the twentieth century. One of the beautiful aspects of Wilson's arrangement of the track is his use of a simple quarter note rhythm. One can easily picture Brian sitting at the piano writing "God Only Knows," punching out chords in this rhythm, testing them, and singing the melody out loud. There

> There is more philosophy in one shake of a sleigh bell than in eight measures of words.

is a comfortable common quality in this rhythm (even more so than in the triplet rhythm of "Surfer Girl"), and it displays Brian's tendency toward an R&B-based structure.

Although Brian Wilson, Paul McCartney, and Paul Simon each found initial success by employing straightforward rock and roll rhythms and song structures, each eventually gravitated toward personal impulses:

Recorded by THE BEACH BOYS on Capitol Records
GOD ONLY KNOWS
Words and Music by BRIAN WILSON and TONY ASHER

Wilson to R&B, Simon to jazz, McCartney to the offbeat rhythms of British saloon songs. Wilson's use of a simple rhythm track in "God Only Knows" makes the subtler rhythmic ideas in the melody that much more appealing.

The production too is a lesson in modesty. There are no groundbreaking choices of instruments and no overpowering dynamics; instead there is plenty of evidence of crafty genius in use of the instruments at hand. The careful arrangement of a few favorite instruments (including piano, bass, sleigh bells, wood-percussion, violins, and French horn) and shadings of dynamics that are as subtle as the inflections in the melody yield a track that can stand on its own magnificence. (And it does that very thing on the instrumental album *Stack-O-Tracks*.)

The chords presented on the piano provide, along with the sleigh bells, the quarter-note rhythm. They are arranged into such subtle shadings of harmony that they merge with the invariant tone of the sleigh bells, even as they are in counterpoint with that sound.

Wilson is clever in his use of instruments. The French horn, a rising hopeful figure, is immediately associated with the opening theme but does not reappear until the final tag, producing the sense of a cycle. A martial snare drum figure plays another role in that tag, yielding a sense of finality, of completion.

In the main verses, the sleigh bell-keyboard sounds are voices and support Carl Wilson's lead vocal, while the syncopated bass is a fragile heart, and the lilting violins are the consequences of dreams facing reality (compare with the French horn). All these sounds are mixed in an expert manner to yield as much of a sense of life-experience as can be expected from a three-minute pop song.

The impulses of harmony, melody, and rhythm mentioned thus far are as good a definition of Brian Wilson's art as are those found in any other Wilson song. "God Only Knows" was created at a point in his career – 1966 — when he was moving toward a closing of that phenomenally successful 5-year era of record making (1963-1967). Ten years later Brian emerged from his bedroom to make a few more albums, including the impressive *The Beach Boys Love You*. What was so wonderful about

24

1977's *Love You*, in addition to Brian's actual return, was the return and reaffirmation of his basic instincts in melody, rhythm, and harmony, all very much in evidence in that precious work.

One aspect missing from that 1977 album, however, was the sense of hard-earned perfection in the mixing of sounds, which was a given back in 1966 with "God Only Knows" and *Pet Sounds*. It would seem that Brian Wilson's impulses never left him, but the energy that surrounded the making of "God Only Knows" was qualified by time itself.

Brian allowed Carl Wilson to be mixdown producer for *Love You*, and there is precedent for that: Carl sang the lead on "God Only Knows." On the back of the original sheet music for "God Only Knows" is a statement attesting that Brian chose Carl to sing the lead because "Carl could do the best job, for his voice range fit the song beautifully — and because he is Brian's brother, it almost sounds like Brian."

He does indeed sound like Brian here, with his smooth tenor and special timbre, characteristic of the Wilson clan. Carl Wilson's lead vocals on "God Only Knows" and "Good Vibrations" are surely the highest peaks of his singing career.

To hear Brian Wilson singing, you must listen carefully to the vocal counterpoint in the tag of "God Only Knows." He is present, with other Beach Boys, fashioning perhaps the most famous of Brian Wilson vocal tags. In this beautifully arranged round, the voices that made up the famous Four Freshmen-styled Beach Boy harmony of "In My Room," "A Young Man Is Gone," and all the others, come apart, revealing the individual sounds that Brian was wont to use as instruments.

Voices as instruments, instruments as voices, all as sounds in Brian's head. In the final analysis, "God Only Knows" is just another example of his love affair with sounds. Studying the lyrics reveals that it is his great philosophical love song; but analysis of the sounds leads to the same conclusion. There is more philosophy in one shake of a sleigh bell than in eight measures of words.

Brian Wilson was the boy who taught his brothers to sing harmony at night as they lay in their beds. He was the man who sent people off to

25

record dripping faucets and crashing ocean waves. He is the man who holds the record for wearing out copies of "Be My Baby."

The appreciation of Brian Wilson's personal philosophy, as expressed in his sounds, makes so many of us fans. That is also why, despite the London Symphony Orchestra's omission, I sit back as the road crew prepares the stage for the touring Beach Boys — and hear sleigh bells.

dennis wilson and the spirit of america

By Don Cunningham

(Originally published in March 1984)

Dennis Wilson sits on the floor of the hotel suite watching TV. He turns his head, jumps to the open door, and invites my young sister Tammy and me to come in with a hoarse "Hey, you wanna meet Christie McVie?" He vanishes toward the bedroom. By the time we find the bedroom, he has closed in on McVie on a king-sized bed and is saying "Let's get married." In the process, he spills her drink on the pillow. McVie's reply: "No, let's just have a lifelong affair."

This took place on a March night in 1979, following a Beach Boys performance at Radio City Music Hall. It was just prior to the release of the band's first CBS album, *L.A. (Light Album)*.

When I noted that his composition, "Baby Blue," was the B-side of the latest Beach Boys single and added that I considered it quite beautiful, Dennis responded almost solemnly, "I wrote every note of that." At my mention of Brian, Dennis' eyes lit up, and he became wistful as he stated, "Brian is beautiful. You wanna talk to him?" There was a moment of nervousness for me as Dennis grabbed the telephone and quickly dialed California. I was somewhat thankful that Brian was not at home, then listened as Dennis instructed Brian's housekeeper to be sure that Brian's apartment was clean.

Dennis' attention span was short and his energy enormous. Soon he leapt to the piano (the room had bed, grand piano, and bucket of champagne) and improvised a section of "Heroes and Villains." He beckoned McVie to join him, showing her a bass part to play along with his higher chords. Then he jumped up and danced with my sister as McVie played on.

There is more to the story than a few paragraphs can convey, yet perhaps you sense the restlessness and gentleness of Dennis Wilson as I witnessed them during that brief 45-minute encounter in New York. He could be clumsy, he could ignore the ordinary aspects of conversation, the badinage, yet he was dear, so obviously in love with music and in love with love. He was fine at the piano, although I am sure he had been drinking. We now know he was drinking too much.

You see, it was Dennis Wilson who fell victim to the California myth—not Brian. It was Dennis who lived the dream of a restless, endless, sun-kissed adolescence, until the dream died in the reality that time brings. Brian's problems are of a different sort. They involve a classic conflict between creative genius and societal demands. Dennis' downfall came in the way of heartbreak—and he had a big heart—when it became obvious that to be fully appealing, adolescence must be evanescent. And one must grow up to survive.

In the later years, the economics of the life of the Beach Boys have dictated that they tour often and exploit the appeal in the promises of Brian's early songs—the dream, the myth. Yet none of the others were living that beguiling dream of endless youth, as was Dennis. His pursuit of the dream had to become less viable, even if it worked at times. In concert he could upstage the rest of the band with his untutored, unabashed drumming, and thousands of fans would share in the feeling. He loved performing, yet it became for him a siren, in that it demanded a belief in the myth. In later years, the pleasure of performing and generating the myth must have afforded less and less of a buffer against the shortcomings of an unreasonable lifestyle.

In the restlessness of Dennis' lifestyle, the difficulties of his personal life, the idealism of his performances, and the irony of his death in the Pacific Ocean, I see a microcosm that mirrors modern American culture. He epitomized the good of the culture: the idealism and spiritual freedom, and also the bad: excess, recklessness, and disregard for necessary authority.

To embrace Dennis' memory is to reaffirm our belief in a noble, albeit flawed, American spirit. That Dennis could be emblematic of such basic values is a tribute to the man. That such values could sustain a free

society for more than 200 years is a tribute to the values—even as the reality of life with those values comes not without warnings. We are challenged to live in the tension caused by our freedom's ability to uplift our spirits and, at the same time, confuse and misdirect us through excess. It seems Dennis was meeting this challenge head-on throughout his life.

The press on the Beach Boys seems to be developing into a love affair with the dual fun-fun-fun/drugs-divorce-dissension identity of the band. The press treats this as a phenomenological curiosity. I would hope for a future recognition of the Beach Boys' legacy as a real and brave measure of the merits and flaws of our society. In the meaning of their art and the unfolding of their personal lives lies a sort of dialectic that can serve to strengthen an understanding of our society.

If that is the case, then Dennis Wilson, American and victim of the California myth, along with the other Beach Boys, will stand heroic in alerting us to our cultural behavior. I see this lesson, given to us in the art and lifestyle of Dennis and the Beach Boys, as being much more cogent than the words and theatrical acts of, say, John Lennon.

In death lies hope when others survive to reflect and learn from the life. Thank you, Dennis, for teaching us valuable lessons through your sometimes brave, sometimes foolish, but always heart-motivated acceptance of our cultural passions.

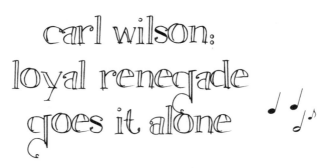

carl wilson: loyal renegade goes it alone

By Colin McEnroe

(Originally published in September 1981)

As Carl Wilson walks through the Howard Johnson's lounge on his way back to his room, the members of his back-up band call out fragments of a long show-biz introduction: "your friend and mine" and "a legend in his own lunch time."

It's one of those running gags that rock bands develop to fill the tedium of road life. The introduction goes on and on, listing credits, heaping plaudits, and building expectations. They never get to the guy's name, of course.

When Carl Wilson himself is introduced later that night at the Hartford Civic Center, it is with the simple invocation: "How about a great big Hartford welcome for Beach Boy Carl Wilson?"

Well, how about it? The Hartford welcome is neither great nor big. If the blinding lights did not pin Wilson to the stage like a butterfly on a mounting board, he would see the sight that all opening acts try not to think about. The seats in the floor sections directly in front of the stage are about one-third full. The crowd is slowly trickling into the coliseum, and hundreds of humans clog the corridors – all too willing to wait in pizza and beer lines rather than listen to the opening band.

If you buy the idea that jokes are often invented to diffuse anxiety, then maybe it's no accident that the band's big joke these days is an introduction. Most of the current dilemmas and ironies in Carl Wilson's career are summed up in the real introduction.

After all, Wilson has courageously decided **not** to be a Beach Boy – at least for a while. Dissatisfied with the group's lack of artistic ambition and disillusioned by a sloppiness creeping into its style, Wilson has temporarily abandoned the other members, most of whom are his relatives.

On the other hand, his name alone does not readily identify him or command attention. What choice does he have but to invoke his past and allow himself to be introduced as a Beach Boy?

Still, the introduction raises questions about Carl Wilson's relationship to the band he worked in for twenty years. When will he return to them? Under what circumstances?

"I miss 'em," Wilson admitted. On July 5, he went back to his hotel room after a gig in Michigan and watched a televised Beach Boys concert, performed on a boat in Long Beach, California.

"It was painful," Wilson said simply.

Wilson recorded his first solo album this year after returning from a Beach Boys tour of Europe.

"It became clear to me that the guys weren't going to go for an album," he said. Wilson even participated in "a little writing seminar" with his bandmates in the hopes of stimulating their creativity. Now he shrugs, "There wasn't any energy in that avenue."

The lack of interest among the other Beach Boys in writing new material and Wilson's belief that the band was touring without adequate rehearsal left him feeling disaffected. To make matters worse, other band members started talking about playing a lot of big club dates in Nevada resort towns like Las Vegas and Lake Tahoe.

"The trouble with those places is that you go down to the showroom around 9:00 each night and you do a real short set because they want to get the crowd out and bring the next group in. It means doing a lot of the old meat-and-potatoes numbers, and you wind up going through the motions."

Even now, one of Carl Wilson's most fervent hopes is that his solo album will "encourage the guys to get moving and write music." Although he currently occupies the role of the renegade, he is still very much a team player for a band that has – during its long, legendary, turbulent and sometimes tragic history – often demonstrated extreme difficulties in behaving like a team.

Carl Wilson has always been widely regarded as the least quirky Beach Boy. The band's psychedelic dalliances in the 1960s are virtually public record by now, as are the severe psychological disturbances suffered by Carl's brother Brian, the moody genius who led the band to prominence. The third Wilson brother, Dennis, has been through his share of dark moments, including a brief association with Charles Manson.

> **Carl Wilson has looked, to outsiders, like the man who picked up the slack when others were wrestling with traumas.**

In the 1970s, band members veered off into the New Age self-development disciplines like EST, health food, and TM. There have been breakdowns, departures, declines and ascents.

"The Beach Boys were a microcosm," Wilson said. "We were going through all the same stuff that everybody else was going through."

Through it all, Carl Wilson has looked, to outsiders, like the man who picked up the slack when others were wrestling with traumas.

"My role has often been to suggest that there might be other points of view," Wilson said. "I guess I've been sort of a peacemaker. The history of the Beach Boys has been that whoever's been up to it has anchored the band."

The Beach Boys happened to Carl Wilson at an age when few people feel particularly anchored. He was 14 when the band was formed in Hawthorne, California; 15 when the first hit single "Surfin'" came out.

"I was so young I didn't know what I was taking on," Wilson said. "How could anyone know? One Saturday afternoon Dennis and Michael (Love, the Wilsons' cousin) came back from the beach and told us we were going to form a band and play music about the beach and cars."

It was a modest proposal, with immodest results. The three Wilson brothers, their cousin Mike Love, and their friend Al Jardine became one of the most potent commercial music forces in the world, spawning countless imitators. More importantly, this surf-and-car band was a catalyst, triggering the writing career of Brian Wilson, a shy young man who emerged as an American rival to the Beatles in a race to create pathbreaking, sophisticated pop music.

In 1966, the unspoken competition between Brian Wilson and Lennon and McCartney reached its peak, with the release of the Beach Boys' *Pet Sounds* and the Beatles' *Revolver*. In a recent interview with *Musician* magazine, Paul McCartney admitted that *Pet Sounds* was the biggest influence on the Beatles when they began to make *Sgt. Pepper's Lonely Hearts Club Band*.

Pet Sounds suggested a burgeoning sophisticated talent that recalled, in some ways, the early career of the greatest American popular music composer, George Gershwin.

"God, Brian loves Gershwin," Carl Wilson confided. "He used to play 'Rhapsody In Blue' over and over. He even did a special arrangement of it."

The sequel to *Pet Sounds* was to be *Smile*, a much heralded collaboration with Van Dyke Parks, and Brian's most ambitious project to date. The album was never completed. Some of the laboriously assembled vocal tracks were wiped blank, apparently in an impulsive gesture of despair by Brian, whose mental state had deteriorated.

The mention of the incident causes Carl Wilson to wince from remembered anguish. He seems reluctant to discuss it.

"Brian was so sensitive," he says finally, hesitantly. "He was such a... delicate balance. He was just the wrong person to go popping LSD."

Brian stopped touring with the band, and Carl inherited the job of singing the deliciously whiny falsetto lead vocals on songs like "Don't Worry Baby" and "Wouldn't It Be Nice." In 1971, he first demonstrated an interest in taking on the mantle of composer as well. His first composition, "Long Promised Road," was one of the more interesting cuts on the *Surf's Up* album and was released as a single, but it only reached number 89 on the *Billboard* chart.

Ten years later, Carl Wilson has stepped out from Brian's prodigious shadow. He is not the genius his brother once was, but his new music is far more interesting than anything Brian Wilson has offered his fans over the last five or six years.

His decision to break free of the band has left the Beach Boys in a state of mild disarray. When the Beach Boys came to Hartford a month ago, Brian tried to resurrect his adenoidal falsetto and become a lead vocalist once again. What came out of his mouth sounded like the last throes of a little deuce coupe with a cracked flywheel. His falsetto had vanished by his second or third number, and by the time "Good Vibrations" rolled around, Brian was singing only the low notes, holding back while intermittent Beach Boy Bruce Johnston chimed in on the unreachable upper register. There is, it turns out, a certain irony to that arrangement.

> "Now that I'm alone, I really respect the hell out of what Michael does for the Beach Boys."

"When we recorded 'Good Vibrations,' I sang most of the lead vocal, but Brian did the high notes because I couldn't hit them," Carl remembered. "As time went on, my voice got stronger, and I had no trouble doing them in concert."

When told of the band's concert troubles, Carl sighed and muttered, "Some rehearsals would help a whole lot."

When Carl Wilson took the Hartford Civic Center stage in his role as the opening act for the Doobie Brothers, he didn't seem to know what to say to the crowd or how to say it. Mike Love does most of the talking at Beach Boys concerts. Wilson launched into some of the surprisingly hard-rock-

36

ing tunes from his solo album, slipping two Beach Boy oldies, "Darlin'" and "Long Promised Road," into the repertoire. His voice sounded strong, whether crooning characteristically through his new single "Heaven" or roaring raucously through "The Right Lane" and "Bright Lights" – songs that seem to draw inspiration from the Rolling Stones and Bad Company.

The crowd listened politely, but there were none of the huge ovations to which the Beach Boys are accustomed. The crowd had come to see the Doobie Brothers, and Carl Wilson was in the unusual (for him) position of having to win over someone else's audience. For the first time in years, he's been getting butterflies before shows.

"I kind of like it," he said. "It's a new challenge. To do a Beach Boys show, all you have to do is show up."

Still, he's suddenly, painfully aware of the roles played by his fellow Beach Boys.

"Now that I'm alone, I really respect the hell out of what Michael does for the Beach Boys, what all the guys do," he said. "It's like – what's wrong with this picture? The guys aren't there, that's what's wrong."

The Doobie Brothers have asked Wilson to stay on as opening act for the second leg of their summer tour, which would keep him working well into the autumn. Somewhere in there, he must begin discussing the possibility of a new album with the Beach Boys. He thinks they will agree to do one, but there's a subtle air of resignation lingering behind his words.

Perhaps Carl Wilson is owning up to the fact that the golden days of the Beach Boys, when every note crackled with creative excitement, soared with bittersweet bliss or quivered with wrenching dolor, are over.

"Maybe the group is into a habit," he said. "Back when we were recording a lot, it seemed like every day was sacred. That feeling has not been present with the group for a while."

good vibrations

By Don Cunningham

(Originally published in March 1980)

In concert, that first protracted word by Carl is a killer. Brian probably figured it that way all those years ago. His younger brother was a teenager when Brian chose him to sing lead on his most ambitious opus, his "pocket symphony." Into the Age of Aquarius, out front of the Beatles, forging a road for his "group," Brian had guts. He was tuned into a great heavenly source of power. He had a deep-down feeling that he could do it all. Let's have little brother Carl sing this one. Sixties justice.

Of course, the reason more often stated for choosing Carl to sing lead on "Good Vibrations" is that he had the more R&B-flavored voice, and "Good Vibrations" would be a progressive R&B song. Yes and yes. When the first verse of the song soars along its sophisticated lyrical path, Carl's strong but passive tonal quality breathes life and familiarity. As a result, the listener is comfortable with the adventure.

"Good Vibrations" begins with Carl joined by a staccato organ rhythm. A sense of drama is immediately felt. A muted bass underneath joins in with a counter melody. Then the organ is mixed down, leaving Carl and the bass, which soon are joined by drums, tambourine, and wind instruments. The woodwinds descend mysteriously until bass and drums cause a shift in direction and momentum, pushing into the chorus.

The chorus creates a strong resolution. While the opening lyrics offered evidence in the forms of sun, hair, words, and colors, the opening music was like a series of metaphysical questions that have to be resolved. Resolution comes in the way of a Mike Love bass vocal statement followed by traditional Beach Boys phrasing—bop bop—and harmony (traditional in arrangement and repetitive use). As if to say the answers have been with us all along, the group sings "Surfin' U.S.A." harmonies behind the "good, good, good" hook, emphasizing it by rising upward.

The bottom line is that you can't and you shouldn't try to separate "Good Vibrations" from "Surfin' U.S.A." or most of the things Wilson has done. It's all of a piece; Brian's answer and the way he says it; a celebration.

The overlay for the traditional Beach Boys vocal in the chorus includes cello and theremin, creating a tension. The effect is less psychedelic than metaphysical or spiritual, foreign sounds wrapping around those that are more familiar. Verse and chorus come around twice (although slightly altered the second time) and provide a non-intimidating ABAB start to the song. The whole structure is as follows: A-B-A-B-C-D-B(part)-E(part of C)-coda(part of B).

The C section deserves to be labeled the "psychedelic" element. Here an assortment of instruments provides fragments of earlier themes, inverted and syncopated, giving the listener a sense that the song is traveling backward. This musical confusion accompanies '60s-style sentiments in the lyric: "I don't know where, but she sends me there...what a sensation."

40

But that section stops abruptly, and a slowed-down religious figure takes over. A meditative organ spells chords behind a tambourine beat (Dear Lord). A heart-thumping bass jumps in to restate the progression. There is Brian's delicate falsetto on "Gotta keep…"—the only teenager from the choir, lingering in church, questioning. The choir enters—as the Beach Boys: "Good, good, good…" Again, Brian's best answer.

Lest Brian wax too serious, the song moves into the "Na na na na na" section, speaking at once joy and self-effacement. Finally, the cello and theremin take a bow before tambourine, bass, et al. fade the song out.

"Good Vibrations" is a song with which Brian consciously defends his personal philosophy of songwriting. Repeatedly, "heavier" musical elements are joined with Brian's own pet sounds, resulting not in tension, but resolution. Brian's sounds are as "heavy" as you care to make them out to be; but that doesn't really matter. What matters is Brian Wilson, his soul, and his sharing of it with us.

> "Good Vibrations" is a song with which Brian consciously defends his personal philosophy of songwriting.

The adjective complex is often used to describe "Good Vibrations" in a way that misleads. At many points in the song, instrumentation is reduced to only a few pieces, or there is a single voice or no voice. If the song is complex, it is because so much is contained in individual instrumental lines and voices. Simply, the song approaches its meaning in affective and effective ways.

Over a period of six months in 1966, Wilson produced dozens of fragments and alternate complete versions of "Good Vibrations." Some have surfaced and reveal him experimenting with instruments and rhythmic themes on his way to the final version. It would be unwise to analyze those fragments, because we can't know how seriously they were considered. The final version is the work Brian gave to his public, and so he must be judged by that. Of great interest, however, is an oft-quoted statement by Brian's chief engineer at the time, Chuck Britz, who has said the final version sounded most like the version Brian nearly completed early in the sessions. Which leads me to conclude that if the whole experience was an experiment, a confidence lesson, Brian eventually trusted his immediate, earlier instincts.

There have been no worthwhile cover versions of "Good Vibrations" over the years. Todd Rundgren's 1976 single was a note-for-note, pure flattery imitation, which paled nevertheless in comparison. A dreadful 1975 recording by the British group The Troggs makes the recent Sunkist commercials shine. "Good Vibrations" is high art to such an extent that to cover it is either to copy it or parody it. No artist will gain in attempting to add to the expression of the original artist.

a children's song

By Don Cunningham

My heart leaps up when I behold
  A rainbow in the sky:
So was it when my life began;
So is it now I am a man;
So be it when I shall grow old,
  Or let me die!
The child is father of the Man;
And I could wish my days to be
Bound each to each by natural piety.

Wordsworth lived to the ripe age of 80. Born in the spring; died in the spring; and spring (or youth, or the child) was a point of reference for his art. The joy a child feels might be called unspeakable except that Wordsworth and artists like him have summoned it. To the end his heart leaped up.

As did (and does) the heart of Brian Wilson. Wilson was born on the last day of spring, the day before summer — so people can be forgiven for believing his music is about summer. In fact, Wilson's music is anchored in qualities of spring: freshness, renewal, blithe spirits—in a word, youth. Like Wordsworth's poetry.

Is the inner child the greatest muse? Perhaps it is characteristic of great artists that they address, consciously or subconsciously, both experiences first met in youth and feelings first expressed in youth. The genuine unadorned articles. Impulses from a vernal wood. From the warmth of the sun. Perhaps it is in using motifs of youth that an artist makes great art speak to and for a culture and makes it resonate as great art resonates—to set us dreaming, as Flaubert said. Without those unembellished, universal motifs, a work will fall short of such powers, soon becoming dated, uninspiring. We see enough of that.

More than 30 years after he began creating it, Brian Wilson's music appears to be standing the test of time. It does not sound dated; it con-

tinually inspires listeners and influences new artists. There is a classicism in it. I wonder how that classicism relates to what might be called the "children's music" contained within.

> "I heard the word
> Wonderful thing
> A children's song"

Let's look at the relationships between children's songs and Wilson's work. Consider two categories: (1) his recordings of well-known children's songs in whole or in part and (2) his creation of novel melodic and rhythmic conceits that themselves have the character of children's songs.

As for the first category: Wilson recorded an upbeat "Ten Little Indians" and a sloppy "Patty Cake (Baker Man)" when the Beach Boys were just starting out. Although Capitol Records (and Nick Venet) might have been part of the stimulus for those tracks, I believe the songs would not have been recorded if Brian had no interest in them.

Two years later (1965, for the *Summer Days* album), when his creative efforts were in high gear and he had a reputation to uphold, Wilson was not averse to recording "Baa Baa Black Sheep" (or "Twinkle Twinkle Little Star") in the form of "And Your Dream Comes True." In fact, on the *Summer Days* album he reached back to both a song from early youth and a song from late youth (Phil Spector's "Then He Kissed Me"). In 1966, Wilson used a bit of "Frère Jacques" in "Surf's Up." In the early 1970s he mixed "Here Comes Santa Claus" into "Child Of Winter" and added "Starlight

> Wilson was born on the last day of spring, the day before summer – so people can be forgiven for believing that his music is about summer.

Starbright" to a version of "This Whole World" produced for his wife and sister-in-law (Spring). Around 1977 he recorded the whole of "Shortenin' Bread."

One must conclude that children's songs were and are a constant presence in Brian's musical vocabulary. In fact, his personal treatment of "Shortenin' Bread" seems never to go away. Listen for it in "Ding Dang," "Too Much Sugar," "Metal Beach," and, most recently, "Fantasy Is Reality (Bells of Madness)." Incidentally, I cannot pursue here a category of instances in which Brian was influenced directly by children's songs when writing new music. It is a matter of a lack of evidence—although writer David Leaf reported that Brian admitted to being inspired by "When You Wish Upon a Star" during the writing of "Surfer Girl."

Brian Wilson's use of children's songs, directly or in altered form, illustrates his unapologetic regard and need for that kind of music. He relishes the fat, easy cadences and repetition in children's songs. He recognizes the merits of their stepwise melodies and clockwork rhythms. By actually recording them, he gives us this clue: he will get to where he wants to go with his art by traveling through that music, not around it; certainly not by avoiding it. Like other great artists, Wilson knows instinctively that this is the proper path. Mahler followed this path when he incorporated Frère Jacques into his first symphony. Other examples abound.

Then there is the second category: original music. It seems to be a rule that a great composer is allowed to have one of his works enter the pantheon of famous children's songs. There are Brahms' "Lullaby," Foster's "Oh Susanna," Richard Rodgers' "My Favorite Things," and Mozart's "Twinkle Twinkle Little Star" melody. In Brian Wilson's case, the jury is still out, but "Little Saint Nick" and "In My Room" would seem to be contenders.

> Listen to "Surf's Up" where Brian sings "Are you sleeping, Brother John?" and think, ah yes, a children's melody.

Why does that happen? Certain subject matter, cadences, rhythms, and overall singability add up to a timeless treasure that children can appreciate. Each case of a children's song cited in the last paragraph is evidence of the composer's understanding of the power and legitimacy in such constructions.

Go farther. Consider the children's music that likely will never be referred to as such. Listen to "Surf's Up" where Brian sings "Are you sleeping, Brother John?" and think, ah yes, a children's melody. Then hold that thought and apply it equally when Brian sings "The laughs come hard in auld lang syne." It is a children's melody and then some. Or sing "Please don't let me argue any more" (from "Kiss Me Baby") or "As long as there are stars above you" (from "God Only Knows").

Can we reach the conclusion that Brian Wilson's songs are children's songs? Yes, in a sense, but that is another way of saying that his music is serious classical music—stirring the youthful angels of our natures. The same can be said of other great musical artists. "You're So Good To Me" is a children's song, but so are "Beautiful Dreamer" and "Eine Kleine Nachtmusik," and so on. It comes back to the definition of classicism: something having to do with defining a culture's noble purposes and capabilities in a way that endures, remains fresh, is beloved. Wordsworth's poetry. Wilson's music.

fifteen bigger ones

By Tom Ekwurtzel

(Originally published in September 1981)

The release of the well-received *Capitol Years* British box set has called more attention to Brian Wilson's constant wave of quality productions. I'd like to take a closer look at Brian's work – with a more defined, less clichéd view.

Here's my premise: I've taken each of the band's albums from Capitol's *Surfin' Safari* to Reprise's *Surf's Up* (excluding the *Concert* and *Party* albums) and chosen one song which best represents the growth and personality of Brian Wilson. I came up with the following list, which I believe has some interesting features. No hits are on this list; I've considered only album cuts.

1. *Surfin' Safari*: "Chug-A-Lug"

It's a cute biographical thing: Brian with his radio; Dennis with motor engines; Carl with food; David Marks even gets a portrait. There is definitely some Brian Wilson philosophy in those lyrics, and Brian's organ solo signals greater things to come.

2. *Surfin' U.S.A.*: "Farmer's Daughter"

This became a classic Brian Wilson melody (and song) although it should be mentioned that "Finders Keepers" also showed some completely new patterns and techniques which later appeared in "A Thing Or Two" (from *Wild Honey*), "Gettin' Hungry" (from *Smiley Smile*) and other songs.

3. *Surfer Girl*: "Catch A Wave"

A ballad would be the most obvious choice but the good ones (the title track, "In My Room") were hits and "Surfer Moon" and "Your Summer Dream" missed the mark a bit. On "Catch

A Wave," the harp run is brilliant, and the chord change in the chorus (from D — "Catch a" to F –"wave") may have been a first in rock.

4. *Little Deuce Coupe*: "Car Crazy Cutie"

Here Brian makes an obvious acknowledgment of Dion. "A Young Man Is Gone" would be a good second choice.

5. *Shut Down Volume II*: "Keep An Eye On Summer"

We had to have a ballad sooner or later. This gem is sandwiched between great hits ("The Warmth Of The Sun," "Don't Worry Baby," "Why Do Fools Fall In Love") and awful duds ("Louie Louie," "Shut Down, Part II," "Cassius Love vs. Sonny Wilson"). If Carl could explain those chords at the fade out, he'd be another Hindemith.

6. *All Summer Long*: "Don't Back Down"

Perhaps the title track should get the nod, but "Don't Back Down" is the real ending to the surfing stage. The chords and progressions are so simple, while the background harmonies are so lush and complex. From here on in, everything is complex: chords, melody, harmony, bass lines. When I was young and learning guitar, I was playing along with Jagger/Richards, not Brian. Otherwise, I would have had to drop it right here.

7. *Today*: "She Knows Me Too Well"

Or "Kiss Me Baby" or "Please Let Me Wonder" or "Don't Hurt My Little Sister" or... Production-wise, *Today* was a concept album. What a sound. Even the duophonic rechanneling couldn't destroy it. "She Knows Me Too Well" takes everything on the album and, after all these years, becomes the focal point on side two. I rate *Pet Sounds* higher than this album only because of the final "Bull Session" cut.

8. *Summer Days (And Summer Nights!!)*: "Let Him Run Wild"

Everyone should agree with this choice, although "Salt Lake City" and "Amusement Parks U.S.A." are two real gems. However, they have nothing like the jazzy innovations of "Let Him Run Wild," which strongly telegraphs what would be coming up in later albums.

9. *Pet Sounds*: "I Just Wasn't Made For These Times"

I can argue this. I really can. You see, they could have made this the title track of the album and got no argument. Second choice is "Here Today." Third choice: "You Still Believe In Me."

10. *Smiley Smile*: "Vegetables"

This isn't as difficult as you might think. Everything else sounds like bits and pieces. "Veggies" was concise, complete, and full of life and imagination.

11. *Wild Honey*: "Aren't You Glad"

Brian's lighthearted trip into R&B is best represented here with the light Motown riff. "Country Air" is, of course, a magnificent song too, but I feel it isn't what *Wild Honey* is about in the strictest sense. Brian was in need of respite in '67 and "Aren't You Glad" was probably knocked out as casually as it still sounds today.

12. *Friends*: "Busy Doin' Nothin'"

The notes, scales, and chords are just so wild on this blissful Brian opus. When has ennui been so well stated in rock? He spends an entire verse trying to phone someone, and ends up writing him; spends another verse giving the listener detailed directions to Bellagio Road. A great big piece of Brian. Philosophy and Samba.

13. *20/20*: "I Went To Sleep"

This is almost "Busy Doin' Nothin', Part II." A friend of mine thinks "Sleep" is 100% cocaine – written during, for, and about a cocaine high. A sleepy tune, certainly, and a reflection of Brian at the time. "Time To Get Alone" is a close second.

14. *Sunflower*: "This Whole World"

Here comes Brian, hooking and juking with this tremendous accomplishment. Time makes this album better, but "This Whole World" sounded brilliant on the first listen. Typical of overall form, the tune states its case and splits, short and sweet.

15. *Surf's Up*: "'Til I Die"

To me, this was the end of an era the way "'Don't Back Down"
was the end of an era. When the guys didn't really care for it,
that was it. No more from Brian. No more 100% effort. "'Til I
Die" was telegraphing. Brian was in effect saying "this band
will be. I will be (without them), set for life with royalties and
Sunkist, and bored as hell."

I can't consider anything after *Surf's Up* on my list. What's the point?
It's not Brian's band anymore.

15 Bigger Ones. Put them on a cassette and give it a listen. It's action-
packed, without a second's rest – the way big brother Brian used to
churn 'em out.

why do fools fall in love

By Don Cunningham

(Originally published in March 1979)

In the film *American Hot Wax*, Alan Freed was depicted giving a side-walk audition to an ersatz Frankie Lymon and the Teenagers. A person listening to Lymon's 1956 recording of "Why Do Fools Fall In Love" could be struck by the notion that such an encounter might actually have occurred, and a tape recorder might have been present. The sound of Lymon's recording is that rough. Yet it is rough in a very good way. It is that precious primitivism, that celebration of human voice and spirit known as doo-wop. Doo-wop was a timeless genre that avoided strings, percussion, overdubs, and more. The sound was real. Vocals produced all the feeling that was necessary; excessive production would only undermine the sentiment.

Of course, one might lift the song entirely from the genre and set it down in a completely different musical environment, say mid-Sixties L.A. rock and roll. In 1964, Brian Wilson created an unabashed rock version of "Why Do Fools Fall in Love" which did no injustice to Lymon's version and now stands alongside it in terms of creative success and in our collective memory.

Young Frankie Lymon helped write "Why Do Fools Fall In Love," and for him that would prove to be a stroke of genius. The song remains today an exemplar of a musical age. Yet, as society would have it, Lymon's career was expendable. He died tragically and too soon.

It is instructive to contrast these two recordings. In adapting someone else's material, Brian Wilson revealed the machinations of his early, Spector-influenced thought process. Wilson did not rewrite the song, but he transformed it. Those were the days when, if the Beach Boys covered an oldie, it was a total redefinition of the song. How we long for that state of affairs today, in light of *15 Big Ones* and *M.I.U. Album*.

51

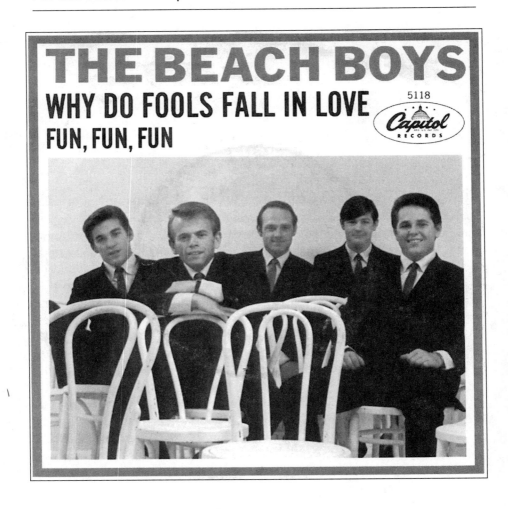

Both versions appear to be in the key of F-sharp, which is not easy to work with instrumentally. It could be that either is a speeded-up key of F, especially the Beach Boys case, which features many more instruments. Of great interest are the introductory "doom-bas," because they are an instance of Wilson altering the original structure significantly. Lymon immediately establishes a secure tonic, as the bass voice drops to low F-sharp, then wanders upward. In Wilson's opening, the tonic is nowhere to be seen (heard), and the listener must wait for the following "ooh-wahs" to find the key. Wilson's opening is roughly Lymon's turned upside down.

To further heighten the excitement here, Wilson seemingly speeds up the tempo by firmly dividing some notes into half-beats. A philosophy of "making it fun" starts to become evident at this early point. One might check the differences between the Beach Boys' single version and album version (yes, there were differences as early as 1964). On the album track, a sharp drum slap replaces Lymon's "yeah." On the single, Wilson eliminates the first beat and places a dense, ethereal vocal harmony around the bass statement.

> Those were the days when, if the Beach Boys covered an oldie, it was a total redefinition of the song.

Lymon's version has a great jazz-tinged bass guitar supporting the melody of the A sections. Wilson's version has a more pop-oriented three-note bass, which frequently is joined by a vocal chorus. This is an example of Wilson opting for the impact of an overall sound texture rather than the excitement of a single instrument. And that is what Brian Wilson and Phil Spector are all about. "Why Do Fools Fall In Love" might be labeled in an oversimplified manner as "Lymon meets Spector."

The original Lymon production features standup bass, simple drum-beat, a standard sax figure, and faint, impromptu-sounding background vocals. Brian uses stronger percussion, with handclaps and something like castanets; introduces a rhythm guitar; and, naturally, comes on strong with backing vocals. In early 1964 this represented Wilson's most ambitious (and Spectorian) production. At that point in time, Wilson had only the *Surfer Girl* and *Little Deuce Coupe* albums to his producing credit.

The listener is advised not to attempt to choose the better of these two versions of "Why Do Fools Fall In Love." In both cases, the artists were extremely successful in accomplishing what they set out to do. Frankie Lymon, with his precious boy-soprano lead vocal and bare, doo-wop setting, earned the biggest hit of his career. Wilson's stronger 21-year-old falsetto complemented a burgeoning production sound and took a big leap in creativity.

In 1975, California Music, the Terry Melcher/Bruce Johnston/Curt Becher team, coaxed a somnolent Brian Wilson into a studio to cut a completely new version of "Why Do Fools Fall In Love." Set in a lower key of D-flat for a Melcher vocal, this track is notable for its driving, Spectorian production. A soulful female voice joins Melcher on the verses, and Wilson's rough voice can be heard in the chorus ("why, why, why, why..."). Although it has a strong beat and neat percussion, the song loses momentum halfway through, giving the impression that Wilson, the producer, didn't quite finish it. Yet this experience might have been important in terms of getting him back in the studio with the Beach Boys the following year.

Our mutual friends

By Don Cunningham

(Originally published in September 1980)

Having accosted Brian Wilson prior to a concert this year, I was struck for some time afterward by the poignancy of his demeanor and by the meaning of it. In many ways Brian has the instincts he always had. That is hopeful and gratifying. The humor, humility, concern, and lack of sophistication are intact. When I mentioned *Add Some Music* to him, his eyes lit up in that boyish way even as he receded somewhat. "Do you have a copy on you?" he blurted. His orange, arty bush of a beard complemented an eager mind. Yet his gross motor movements told a different story, with abrupt, nervous turns reminding me of the tragic loss in confidence and seemingly lost ability to synthesize songs to completion.

In 1966, Wilson guessed he wasn't made for the times, so he created music that producers and songwriters in 1980 have yet to surpass in terms of lyricism, textures, and artistic vision. But Brian Wilson in 1980? The tracks he lays down these days contain typical Brian Wilson sounds and impulses, yet their commercial success is negligible.

In 1865, Charles Dickens, in the late period of his career, sustained the criticism of Henry James, who was prompted by the release of Dickens' *Our Mutual Friend* to proclaim the great wrong of applying to Dickens the status of one of England's great novelists. Today we can enjoy the virtues of *Our Mutual Friend* along with Dickens' other works in the absence of flak such as James'. In the same way, I believe that one day, with little dissent, we will revel in the joyous sounds of the undervalued "Hey Little Tomboy" along with "Wouldn't It Be Nice" and the others.

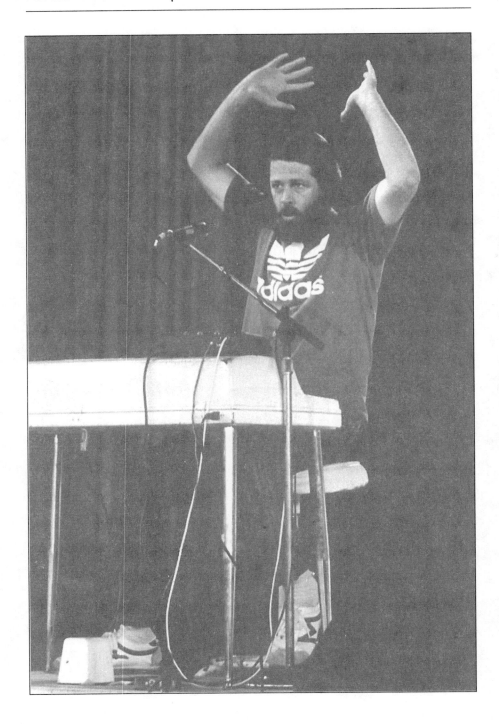

euphoria with hindsight

the beach boys live, june 6-7, 1980

By Andrew G. Doe

(Originally published in June 1980)

Before getting down to business, I must make one thing clear: these Wembley Arena shows were my first live Beach Boy gigs, so if objectivity sometimes takes a back seat...well, you've been warned.

Viewed as a whole, the Wembley shows presented a microcosm of the prevailing scene apropos le Beach Boys – an impeccably presented and performed concert, rooted firmly in the past and with just enough hint at the undercurrents which every now and then threaten to destroy the band. On these nights, euphoria with hindsight may be a more considered approach.

The music itself blended into an emotionally satisfying whole. The program was basically the standard U.S. show, plus "Cottonfields" (top ten here in England in 1970). The past ten years were represented by the aforementioned song, "Rock And Roll Music," "Good Timin'," "Lady Lynda," "School Days," "Some Of Your Love," and the title cut from the latest album *Keepin' The Summer Alive*.

Surprisingly, "Good Timin'" emerged as the worst performed song over two nights, starting almost by accident on the first night. Conversely, and by mutual acclaim, the standout on both nights was Al Jardine's "Lady Lynda" by virtue of the now standard but still truly magical a capella tag, and "spontaneous" reprise ("oooh, that's so good – let's do it again"). "School Days" was presented sans the a capella intro, which I am led to believe is not a bad thing, and all three songs from *Keepin' The Summer Alive* came across as faithful repros of the album cuts.

With the music flowing so uniformly, it was the odd (as in odd-funny and odd-strange) moments that lodged in the mind: Carl, Al, and Eddie Carter doing their guitar-hero bit during "Keepin' The Summer Alive;" the high-kicking chorus line during the encore; Dennis all but falling over the wires and dancing atop the white baby grand – and actually smiling at Mike; Bruce's little message to Nick Kent; the continual shunting of musicians to and fro; the ever-present smokescreen above Brian's baby grand.

Ah, Brian. Now what is there to say? That he continued to water the legend? That he seemed mentally to be on another plane? That perhaps he shouldn't have been there at all? The signs are contradictory, yet encouraging. It was obvious that he wasn't being forced to do something he didn't want to do. When Sumako, Harriett and Lynda tried to entice him into the chorus line on the first night, Brian was having none of it. At the same time he's just not with it at all: looking stunned when Al began "Cottonfields;" forgetting he had to sing the middle eight of "Surfer Girl," until it was too late to remove the cigarette; walking across the stage during "Heroes and Villains." Except during "Good Vibrations," when he added a beautiful and, to me, totally new piano phrase, he played what could best be described as "rhythm" piano. It's been suggested that Brian needs something to occupy his mind and gigs are the easiest way out. A tenable theory.

Nevertheless, it was obvious to all that if Brian had just stood center stage and done nothing, the crowd would have applauded. Every note, however hoarse, and each half-formed gesture was greeted with rapturous applause. The rest of the band willingly accepted their subsidiary roles with good humor, all of which added to the general bonhomie. After all the rumors, it was a great joy to see Dennis. Even more so as he was evidently enjoying himself, looking a little wasted but happy. Carl, considering he was suffering from a nasty dose of food poisoning, was nevertheless congenial Carl. Bruce was nicely unobtrusive. Al was Al.

> It was obvious that if Brian had just stood center stage and done nothing, the crowd would have applauded.

Mike was Mike, although slightly subdued on the first night. Supporting musicians Eddie Carter, Bobby Figueroa, Mike Meros and Joe Chemay did their usual excellent jobs, with Meros' synthesizer lines during "In My Room" being of special note.

In light of the sustained excellence of the performances, it seems unfair to pick holes, yet the content was somewhat predictable. "You Are So Beautiful," "Marcella," and a track from *Holland* would have been very welcome. But again, how many bands can get the fans (ages 10 to 40-plus) dancing in the aisles after but five songs – all those songs being at least ten years old. God bless America.

© Andrew G. Doe

album review:
ten years of harmony

By Tom Ekwurtzel

(Originally published in February 1982)

G ood timin': Three weeks before Christmas, and the Beach Boys release their "greatest tracks of the '70s" double LP, just in time for the holiday buying public. That's not bad for a band that once released a Christmas single on Christmas Eve.

The album is both justly and ironically called *Ten Years Of Harmony,* and it features 29 cuts: 24 from the group's nine studio albums of that decade, plus one song from Dennis Wilson's solo album, two unreleased tracks, one soundtrack rarity, and one live track from the 1974 *In Concert* LP.

This is a generous portion of Beach Boys music. Even for someone who's heard these songs hundreds of times, it is a celebration. For the unfamiliar, this could prove to be a Pandora's box, leading the uninitiated into a large, enigmatic library of works from 1970 to 1980.

With only one real hit in ten years, and no definitive way to choose the right songs, one would figure that 29 choices would yield some bad edges. But the selections are actually well thought out. Thank goodness they've passed on material such as "Goin' South" and "Lookin' At Tomorrow (A Welfare Song)." "Almost Summer" isn't here, which is too bad. Even though the music is consistently wonderful, it would have been nice if the fourth side was filled with unreleased stuff.

But that's not such a big deal when these four sides are chock full of our boys at their best. I believe the Beach Boys' days as a consistent, orthodox, rock entity are long gone, but this collection shows that they continue to add to a handsome resume, even if the gems have become fewer and farther between.

It's interesting that one third of the cuts are from the 1970-1971 albums *Sunflower* and *Surf's Up*. From the former, "Add Some Music To Your Day" sounds, as ever, like enough harmony to fill up ten years all by itself. Also included are the sweet Bruce-Brian collaboration "Deirdre"; one of those uncelebrated masterpieces by the master, "This Whole World"; and the single version of "Cool, Cool Water."

Surf's Up is represented by no less than six tracks, including the title track and "'Til I Die," which very fittingly closes the collection. Personally, I'm not so sure about the inclusion of "Don't Go Near The Water," but "Disney Girls" certainly belongs. A lot of people think this Bruce Johnston song is the only thing the Beach Boys did between the Sixties and 1976. It's a Beach Boys song because of the harmony. "Long Promised Road" and "Feel Flows," Carl's two semi-classics, feature Jack Rieley's obtuse lyrics. Yes, there once was a man named Jack Rieley who did an admirable job with a nearly impossible task – keeping the Beach Ball rolling.

Highlights of more recent vintage include "It's A Beautiful Day" from the soundtrack of the movie *Americathon*. *Ten Years Of Harmony* features the single version of this suburban rocker, which is one of producer Bruce Johnston's high points. As of this writing, "Come Go With Me," Alan's 1978 remake of the Del Viking's classic, is a real Top 20 hit, undoubtedly proving the wisdom of its inclusion here. "She's Got Rhythm" features Brian's unbelievable, for 1978, vocal. Is this the last time we will hear him sing that way?

As for the unreleased material, "San Miguel" is an old (circa 1969) track written by Dennis, with a strong lead vocal by Carl. So where in Sam's Hill has this cut been? Tremendous.

"Sea Cruise," recorded in 1976, is the second previously unreleased track. Only Frankie Ford can do this Huey "Piano" Smith composition correctly. Brian and Dennis can't come close to the original. But even though there is nothing new brought to the song, I'll still take Brian's patented "roller rink" organ style for what it's worth. And if I had my druthers, I'd have picked Brian and Alan's unreleased "Loop De Loop" instead. If it had to be a Dennis Wilson lead vocal, then I would have picked "It's Tryin' To Say," the Brian Wilson gem from the unreleased *Adult Child*. (I hope you've heard it.)

"River Song" is a good choice from *Pacific Ocean Blue*, Dennis Wilson's moody 1977 solo work, which is a painful look at his life at that time.

The quality of the sound here is beautiful. The remix of "Darlin'" from the *In Concert* LP features brighter highs – it sounds like the microphone is attached right to the high-hat. Much more exciting. With the crystal clear reproduction of "San Miguel," I now feel like I'm listening to a song I never heard before – a much better one. In 1971 I listened to the *Surf's Up* tracks on a modest stereo unit, and the pressing and vinyl quality must have been only OK, because listening to the new pressings in 1981 yields some extremely noticeable differences.

Thinking about sound quality raises some questions: Can I find information on the sleeve concerning whether the sound reassignment is digitally monitored? Is the discomputer used? How has the sound been remixed? Who dunnit? Something is missing here. It turns out a lot is missing – a lot of information.

The packaging is lousy: a cover which is just a lame retreat from the horror show of their last LP, only one picture, and absolutely no information as to who plays what, where and when. For example, nothing here will tell you that Blondie Chaplin sings lead on the wonderful "Sail On Sailor." Besides Brian, Mike, Dennis, Carl and Alan, there is a rich history of people who contributed during these years: Bruce Johnston, Blondie Chaplin, Ricky Fataar, Ron Altbach, Daryl Dragon, Billy Hinsche, Mike Kowalski, Ed Carter, Charles Lloyd, Marilyn Wilson, Steve Douglas, Gary Griffin, Bobby Figueroa, and Jim Guercio, to name a few.

In scrutinizing the band's overall output during this time span, one comes up with a blurred picture. A rookie listening to *L.A. (Light Album)* would have a hard time swallowing "Sumahama," as well as most of the rest of the album. For most people, the *M.I.U. Album*'s "Match Point Of Our Love" and "Belles of Paris" are real turnoffs. Attempts at making new sounds have too often fallen even farther off the mark than have attempts at creating intelligent album titles.

Part of being a die-hard Beach Boys fan is making up clever excuses for these sometimes-embarrassing attempts. More often than not, it is best to stick with the "Brian Wilson as sole artist in the group" rationale.

Even Brian's most quirky pieces ("Johnny Carson," "Shortenin' Bread," "Solar System," "Child Of Winter"), I find totally defendable. However, sometimes I think that only "true" fans should have access to such tracks. Will others understand this music? Not immediately.

But there are no such concerns with this collection. *Ten Years Of Harmony* is a fine sampler which can be enjoyed by any listener. Pick it up for a friend, or for the bum who hasn't stopped giving you grief for sticking with these guys for all these years.

come go with me

By Don Cunningham

(Originally published in February 1982)

Surprise! Although Mike Love and Carl Wilson released solo albums in 1981, Al Jardine had the hit record. As this is being written, "Come Go With Me," a Jardine-Beach Boys project, continues to move strongly up the national charts.

Working within the boundaries of our favorite concept, Jardine had produced this song for the 1978 *M.I.U. Album*. Included more recently in the compilation album *Ten Years Of Harmony* and released as a single, this reworking of the Del Vikings' classic has shot up the charts like nothing since "Rock And Roll Music" in 1976.

Many people take a long time to realize that "Come Go With Me" is by the Beach Boys. A compliment to Jardine perhaps? He has scored a hit with a single that is essentially a Beach Boys record, yet deviates from a sound associated with the group. Those who seek creativity within the group should take note. And note too that "Come Go With Me" contains an ingredient common to every sizable Beach Boys hit: exuberance (or energy? or fun?).

Put a feather in Alan's cap for investing Beach Boy projects that he has supervised with such a quality — reaching back to "Cottonfields." Brian Wilson can create exuberance in a fraction of a bass line or background vocal counterpoint. That has always been a key. Perhaps no other group member has appreciated that more than has Jardine. The success of "Come Go with Me" reminds us that Alan has been most successful in producing songs with that favorable quality of Brian Wilson.

It is why "Surfer Girl" sounds so good over the sound system in the ski lodge. It is why disc jockeys can be heard to say, "It's a cold one today, what do you say we warm up with something by the Beach Boys." Getting happy goes a long way toward warming you up. The Beach Boys are timeless because such a quality, a part of their music, addresses a need that is timeless.

alan jardine:
the rhythms of a craftsman

By Michael Bocchini

(Originally published in September 1981)

Summer 1981. Twentieth Anniversary Tour. Spirit of America. On stage, the psychodrama swirls as if separate parts of an individual personality have become visible in a frenetic experiment of survival. Carl Wilson's absence bears witness, as do Dennis Wilson's tirades and Brian Wilson's sometimes choking vocals. Center stage, Mike Love struts to hold the magic together. In his traditional stage right position, Alan Jardine, whom *Crawdaddy* once called "elfin and unchanging," steadily does his work.

The importance of Alan Jardine to the Beach Boys' sound, and perhaps its psyche, was recognized early by Brian. Alan's stay at dental school ended when he was asked by Brian to embark on the group's first major American tour, and to replace David Marks, who had replaced Alan after the group's early and modest success.

Brian Wilson was creating a lasting metaphor for contemporary America from the momentary icons of the 1960s: surf, cars, and the California youth cult. Alan Jardine's roots were in an older and more established form of American music — folk. In the Beach Boys, Jardine found a vibrant link in the progression of "peoples' music." In Jardine, the group found a link to America's musical past.

Alan Jardine did not become a dominant creative force in the group because of this link. But he did become an important thread in the fabric that is the Beach Boys. Alan brought a perspective to the group's public and private existence. In contrast to the frenzy of Brian's world, Alan

has been a touchstone of personal stability. During the trauma of *Smile*, as Brian tested the outer limits of his personal life and his musical life-blood, Alan was establishing the perimeters of his family life.

If nothing else, Alan Jardine's temperament is tied to the rhythms of craftsmen. And you can sense it in his creations, in the evolvement of songs like "Susie Cincinnati" and "Lady Lynda." For him, music is "like anything else; you follow the rules and the axioms and it'll work." In moments of conflict, Alan shows a willingness to defer to the passions of an artist. On *20/20*, Alan sings the lead on "Cottonfields." The production (by Brian) does not follow the "rules and axioms," as Jardine had strongly wished. It follows the vision of Brian Wilson.

> In contrast to the frenzy of Brian's world, Alan has been a touchstone of personal stability.

Since Alan's alternate production can be found on the single version of "Cottonfields," this struggle of creative temperament takes on startling overtones. The production strongly embraced by Alan, and more strongly rejected by Brian, can be best described as pure Brian Wilson.

On *Carl and The Passions: So Tough*, another conflict arose. In an attempt to translate Robert Frost's "The Road Not Taken" into a song, Alan ran into Mike Love's need to add meditation lyrics, and Carl Wilson's production concepts. What resulted was a beautiful song ("All This Is That") with only the slightest hint of its origin. Gone is the hard edge of Frost's examination of the critical choices which confront man.

On his relinquishing of creative control of his original idea for this song, Alan made this comment: "If somebody's really that inspired to do something, then that's great. Then you work with it instead of fighting it, and it comes out okay." Given Frost's poem and the resulting Jardine-Love-Wilson song, things came out okay, but all this is definitely not that.

These incidents are not the mark of a man without insight. They are emblematic of a man with patience and respect for the artistic vision of a group effort. In "California Saga," from *Holland*, Alan Jardine's importance to the Beach Boys began to manifest itself.

The saga begins in time present. In "Big Sur," Mike Love's lyric first describes the seeming dichotomy of land and sea, and sunset and sunrise. The lyric then introduces a unifying image – the springs which rush from the mountains to join the sea. The images are simple, yet their timelessness proves magnetic. They speak of a unity which modern man neglects.

If Jardine was willing to abandon Robert Frost's hard edge in "All This Is That," he embraced an even harder edge in the choice of a Robinson Jeffers poem ("The Beaks Of Eagles") for the work's second movement, which adds a historical context to the saga. Here, Mike's insight is confirmed in complex, rich images. While Mike speaks eloquently about the serenity of nature, Jeffers speaks of its awesome quality. The long-term stability and unity of nature is punctuated with necessary moments of great violence.

72

Jeffers' eagle endures by accepting these disruptions and by responding to them creatively. From the fragments of a lightning-blasted tree she builds a new nest. Out of the ravages of a forest fire she finds sustenance in scorched meat.

The saga's final movement, "California," pays homage to the California of time present – a California whose popular identity has been influenced by the music of the Beach Boys. From the first line, which speaks of the inspiration of the group's earliest success ("On my way to sunny California"), to the borrowed lyric from Brian's most daring risk, *Smile* ("Water, water, get yourself in the cool, cool water"), to the song's rhythm track (borrowed from "California Girls"), "California" maintains the spirit of joy and freedom which has marked the Beach Boys' most popular efforts, and America's most commonly held vision of California.

> The *M.I.U. Album* revealed an important insight into Jardine's concept of what the Beach Boys should be.

To me, the final two movements of "California Saga" have always seemed to capture the essential relationship between the musical temperaments of Brian Wilson and Alan Jardine. For Brian, that involves testing the limits of popular music at no small risk. For Alan, there is a recognition that he would be a part of a new manifestation of American folk music, which could touch a chord in the American consciousness, and renew and refresh its spirit.

The pair's more recent collaboration on *Keepin' The Summer Alive*'s "Santa Ana Winds," which continues the examination of the timeless themes of "California Saga," shows none of the stress of "Cottonfields," and that development seems to bode well for the future.

The *M.I.U. Album* revealed an important insight into Alan Jardine's concept of what the Beach Boys should be. While Brian Wilson receives credit as *M.I.U.*'s "executive producer," the album is produced by Alan (with Ron Altbach). *M.I.U.* relies on what most people who have grown up in America during the past twenty years would recognize as the Beach

Boys' sound. The consistency of production returns listeners to the era that stretched from the surfin' albums to *Summer Days*, and the effect is a refreshing pause.

To be sure, the images of disco queens, Paris, and tennis matches bespeaks a group which recognizes that time has passed since 1962, but the harmony, the **sound**, reminds the listener that, as in the early efforts, the words to most of the songs are only the means by which the voices of the group could complement the sound of the instrumentation – and capture the voices of those of us who sang along.

Only the inclusion of "Winds Of Change" on *M.I.U.* seems to push Alan's concerns ahead of those of the group, and the result is the album's least interesting cut. This song, a non-Beach Boys composition, forces the listener into a lyric which is a short essay on the timeless value of love as a counterpoint to the never ending "Winds of Change."

When Alan's "Lady Lynda" was included on the *Light Album*, the concern stated in "Winds Of Change" was addressed properly. In the *Surf's Up* track "Lookin' At Tomorrow (A Welfare Song)," Alan sang of the need for love in order to sustain a man's welfare in a harsh modern world. In "Lady Lynda," he personalized this message in a beautiful song dedicated to his wife. The song weaves a tapestry of images of love made more compelling because of the reality upon which they are based.

> "Lady Lynda" illustrates the maturity of love; no teenage fantasy of surfer girls.

"Lady Lynda" illustrates the maturity of love; no teenage fantasy of surfer girls or anxiety over lost love. A man has grown with a woman and has placed his faith in a set of values which do not change capriciously with the passage and tests of time. This love is like spring in its quality of renewal after hard times. This union is characterized as an invitation to join in a universal and everlasting song of love.

Alan Jardine's use of song as the vehicle for an image of love as timeless and as varied as the seven notes upon which all our popular music is based expands the scope of "Lady Lynda" and explains much about the attitude of its composer. The song has no value unless it is shared by friends. Music remains a source of joy when it addresses the needs of people in a given time and place. The needs must be addressed in different forms and with different images in order to provide popular access, but the purpose remains constant.

To answer the needs of man to share, to join, and to become one with and in the music is a calling of the highest order, and one for which, through temperament and talent, the folk singer Alan Jardine is most fit. Perhaps it is this awareness that led Brian Wilson to invite Alan Jardine on a journey which has just celebrated its twentieth anniversary.

sloop john b

By Don Cunningham

(Originally published in August 1982)

Qualities of humility and humor in the face of hardship define a spirit that is contained in any song rightly called a folk song. The "Wreck Of The John B," which dates to early years of this century and goes by many names, is clearly such a song.

The "Wreck Of The John B" or "The John B Sails" or "Sloop John B" can be traced at least to the 1920s. Carl Sandburg had something to do with its acceptance as a popular American folk song when he included it in his anthology *The American Songbook* in 1927. The song's author remains unknown. In the 1950s, the Weavers (featuring Pete Seeger) brought "Sloop" to national attention, and it has been a staple for folk singers and folk groups ever since. A version by the Kingston Trio stands perhaps as the classic folk rendition.

The Kingston Trio: three male voices, one of the more popular folk acts of the 1950s-1960s, Alan Jardine's favorites. The great success of the Trio's versions of folk classics resulted from the excellent qualities of their voices as well as their smart vocal arrangements. Jardine wanted the Pendletones (or whatever the fledgling Beach Boys were called in 1961) to be a folk group. Fortunately and inevitably, Brian Wilson's Beach Boys did not realize Jardine's modest concept. As it turned out, Al had to settle for a rock group with folk influences and a gifted artistic leader with a vision that transcended singular notions of rock or folk or whatever.

Jardine's love for the music of the Kingston Trio and the fact that he suggested to Brian Wilson that he record "Sloop" are not the only evidence that the Trio's version inspired Wilson and helped him to come to terms with the song. Aspects of the Trio's version, especially the movements of the voices, hint at some of the vocal results in Brian's Beach Boys version.

Yet Brian Wilson's "Sloop John B" transcended the Trio's version and all others, and in many ways. It was successfully extracted from the genre of pure folk music; it was given a rock beat; it was given a sumptuous instrumental production that not only distinguished it from folk music, but also approached the genre of "serious" orchestral music.

Before comparing two recordings (Kingston Trio and Beach Boys), it would be instructive to note that both use the title "Sloop John B" rather than the earlier "Wreck Of The John B." The latter evokes the tradition of low-key humor in folk lyrics, playing on the idea of a nautical calamity when the song itself is concerned with a ship's deterioration due to rather domestic circumstances (the ship's cook threw away the grits and ate my corn...). By using the title "Sloop John B," Wilson (and the Trio) surrendered that joke. This was the first clue that they would draw the song away from the humorous intent of folk renditions and bring it elsewhere—to the realm of broader, ambiguous meanings associated with popular song.

Is the song about a boat, the John B? Is it about the boat's voyage? Is it about sailing in general? Is this lyric metaphorical — a fable — or does it document a real event? In the only significant change in wording, where the original stated "this is the worst trip since I've been born," Brian (or another Beach Boy?) substituted the dubious "this is the worst trip I've ever been on." The second meaning of a drug experience, although slight, helps to make "Sloop John B" a different kind of song, one that should not be taken at face value, one that should be searched for evidence of values considerably different from those derived from pure folk versions.

The calypso rhythm of the Trio's recording strikes the listener as a radical departure from the (now) more familiar rock beat of Wilson's arrangement, yet this belies a strong similarity in structure and melody.

The Trio's production is mainly voices, with a soft, undulating bass defining the chords and rhythm. Guitar, banjo, and bongos are pushed way back. In the manner of a typical folk arrangement, the bass line is unobtrusive, although infectious. Emphasis is placed on the vocals, which are rich in tone and expertly construed. The four-note bass theme, repeated over and over, is the appropriate tonic followed by a jump to the fifth, a step to the sixth, back to the fifth, and home again.

A calypso rhythm results from the elongation of each initial tone (the tonic). Such a simple bass figure might have appealed to Brian back in the days of his "surfing songs." In fact, when he covered Frankie Lymon's "Why Do Fools Fall In Love" in 1964, he eschewed an original jazz bass figure in favor of a "surfing" three-note bass. Two years later, Brian was pursuing more creative impulses. His bass line for "Sloop John B" was evidence of a matured prowess in melodic and rhythmic arrangement.

The bass in "Sloop John B" is ever-changing, from a looping syncopated initial appearance, to imaginative jazz-styled modulations in the verses, to fast, heartbeat fuzz tones near the end. It is a colorful main character in the song. Note especially the octave leap when it enters the first verse, from low A-flat to high A-flat (the song is in A-flat), followed by a serpentine plotting between those notes.

Overall, the bass notes have a descending character, and that is important. As the bass moves downward, voices move upward. When Wilson was laying down the instrumental tracks, he used a keen sense of how bass would be a counterpoint to the voices, which would be added later. Unlike guitars and percussion, the bass approximates the timbre of the human voice and appears to relate to the voices in a special way. In Beach Boys songs in general, the bass comes across as a figure descending as voices move upward, especially the falsetto. Brian seemed to understand this winning chemistry early on. [As an example of a Beach Boy song in which the vocals have a descending character, consider "Goin' On," the 1980 Bruce Johnston production of a Brian Wilson song. The harmonies are beautiful, but that special relationship with the bass is absent.]

> Jardine wanted the Pendletones (or whatever the fledgling Beach Boys were called in 1961) to be a folk group.

To further consider Wilson's production of "Sloop John B," it is convenient to listen to the instrumental track alone (from the *Stack-O-Tracks* album). The quip on the sleeve of the British reissue of this album has always impressed me. In attempting to justify the release of instrumental-only tracks for an album's worth of Beach Boys songs, the liner-note writer asked, "Have you ever heard 'Sloop John B' without the vocals?" Enough said. Wilson's backing track for "Sloop" is a tour de force.

79

In recording "Sloop John B," the Kingston Trio recorded a song. In recording "Sloop John B," Brian Wilson, in the manner of Phil Spector, "made a record." In addition, like typical Spector, Wilson made a phenomenal record. The difference between creating a song and creating a record is substantial, and the understanding of this is crucial to an understanding of Wilson's work.

Many of the popular songs co-written by Richard Rodgers and Lorenz Hart became standards. These inspired creations by two gifted and skilled songwriters come across as great art whether performed by Judy Garland, Frank Sinatra, Dion DiMucci, or whomever. Rodgers and Hart created great songs. They happen to be songs written in such a way that creative arrangements of them stand up to critical scrutiny.

When Wilson was in the studio creating "Sloop John B," he was producing a recording, and that production contains the essential ingredients that stand up to critical scrutiny. The same can be said for any Wilson song conceived in terms of total production. The composition includes song, arrangement, and production.

I recall that Brian once was asked whether he thought Phil Spector actually helped to write all his big hits in the early Sixties. Brian's answer was insightful; he said that he always felt Spector had to write those songs for them to turn out the way they did. In other words, "Be My Baby" was written in the studio, under the direction of Spector, as much as it was written on paper by his collaborators, Greenwich and Barry.

The same can be said for "Sloop John B," "Good Vibrations," "Let Him Run Wild" and songs throughout the Wilson canon. Wilson wrote the melodies, the counter melodies, the third and fourth and fifth harmonic vocal parts, the bass part, the tambourine part, etc. When you speak of Mozart creating the "Jupiter" symphony, you don't regard it as a few melodies. Mozart wrote every part, for every instrument. Why should we consider Brian Wilson's music differently?

Here is one reason why it is so difficult for other artists to cover Brian Wilson/Beach Boy songs. It is not enough to sing the lyric, to follow the melody. One must approach the total production of the original recording or risk the loss of the original musical and emotional results.

To cover "Sloop" in a rock style, one would be smart to begin with Brian's flute intro (in the manner of a nautical whistle). Then an array of gentle guitars should weave his special tapestry of sound around the opening chord, with tinkling percussion holding the beat. After a couple of bars, bring in Brian's inspired bass and some sharp snare beats followed by quick cymbal and echo added to the guitars. After a few more measures, increase the dynamics of the guitars and various bell sounds. Introduce more drumming. After a few more measures, bring on the whole army of percussion.

> Mozart wrote every part, for every instrument. Why should we consider Brian Wilson's music differently?

Do it all as Brian did it: everything has an introduction, nothing drops out. Like Ravel's "Bolero," the song is a generating cycle, growing through increasing dynamics and the gradual addition of textural elements.

"Sloop John B" does not have a middle eight. Instead, the middle verse ("So hoist up the John B sails…") is repeated twice more, thereby becoming a chorus of a sort. In the absence of musical plot that a middle eight would offer, Wilson created plot using techniques of arrangement and production. The preceding paragraph cited the progression he achieved using building dynamics in an all-out production assault. He achieved even greater musical plot using the voices of the Beach Boys.

It goes like this: first verse ("We come on the") Brian is singing alone; first chorus verse ("So hoist up") Brian sings lead supported by Alan (Alan sings the tonic A-flat melody while Brian starts on C—a two-part harmony that can still be witnessed in concert); second verse ("The first mate") is surprisingly taken by Mike; second chorus verse ("So hoist up") has a bunch of voices supporting and answering Brian's lead and ends in an a capella counterpoint that is out of this world; third verse ("The poor cook") has Brian singing alone once more but with a light (ethereal) harmony above him — and he gives the final line to Mike ("This is the worst trip"); third chorus verse ("So hoist up") everyone sings and fades.

I have always held a strong sense of "Sloop John B" building to a peak at the a capella counterpoint which ends the second chorus verse. This pivotal spot offers a tremendous feeling of musical urgency, of musical necessity. So that the a capella break seems natural, perfect. Unfortunately, it is evidently too difficult to recreate in concert.

By considering the all-out compositional and production assault that characterizes Wilson's "Sloop John B," we are led to a questioning of the song's folk qualities and to the relationship, in general, between Brian Wilson and folk music. Is it possible to call this highly orchestrated rock song folk music? Certainly not if using a traditional definition. A folk aspect is submerged and is no greater a part of "Sloop John B" than is a rock or jazz or pop or progressive aspect.

The musical sub-genre folk rock existed in and around 1965 and included music by Bob Dylan, the Byrds, the Lovin' Spoonful, and many others. This form implied a lyrical concern sympathetic to the folk tradition but with a richer production sound. Is this where "Sloop John B" fits? Probably not, even if Brian Wilson had folk rock in mind when he produced the track.

82

Wilson's "Sloop" is not a hybrid of music genres, as was folk rock. Rather, it uses various musical forms as influences. This produces a large result that includes the grassroots appeal of traditional folk music, the exciting power of popular music, and the creative depth of serious progressive music. And there are other influences. In this way, and along with most of Brian's successful records, "Sloop John B" created a new and unique genre, which remains unnamed.

For lack of a better name, Brian calls his music "rock." Yet that term is too generalizing, confusing the characterization of songs rather than defining them in a helpful way. Until a unique name surfaces for music that is rock and folk and jazz and pop and progressive and whatever, we must cite each of these forms — as in the case of "Sloop John B."

surfin' u.s.a. and fun, fun, fun

By Don Cunningham

(Originally published in August 1983)

1963's "Surfin' U.S.A." and 1964's "Fun, Fun, Fun" are two Brian Wilson creations which, for many reasons, deserve to be analyzed in the same breath. To an average Beach Boys fan (who could not care less about the unreleased takes of "Good Vibrations," the tonal complexity of "God Only Knows," or the lyrical majesty of "Surf's Up"), "Surfin' U.S.A." and "Fun, Fun, Fun" are examples of quintessential Beach Boys style. Here are easy chord progressions, terrific harmonies, soaring falsetto, a fast rock and roll pace, and especially, the nasal, high-E-flat lead vocal of Mike Love.

Although these two songs nearly sum up the early Sixties manifestation "Beach Boys Music," in fact "Surfin' U.S.A." and "Fun, Fun, Fun" showcase the sounds and impulses of an earlier artist and songwriter, Chuck Berry. Brian Wilson's debt to Chuck Berry can not be any more obvious than in these two Beach Boys smashes, made in Brian's early developmental period. For "Surfin' U.S.A.," he used the music of Berry's 1958 hit "Sweet Little Sixteen," while for "Fun, Fun, Fun" he stole the famous guitar intro from Berry's other Top 10 hit of 1958, "Johnny B. Goode."

Yet the influence of Chuck Berry would go much deeper in Wilson's art. The musical philosophy and essence of Berry's music helped shape, to some degree, Wilson's concept of what his own popular music should be, and it therefore pervaded Brian's work. In 1976, 13 years after "Surfin' U.S.A.," Brian scored a Top 10 hit with a version of Berry's "Rock And Roll Music." That later recording stands as a tribute to a music that helped shape a career's worth of artistic triumphs.

Chuck Berry was a rhythm and blues guitar player who stumbled onto success with "Maybelline," the 1955 hit that contained more of the upbeat qualities associated with what was being called rock and roll than the lugubrious rhythms and tones of classic R&B. Berry rearranged his priorities to accommodate the livelier and more popular rock and roll style, as he wrote and recorded his famous string of rock and roll classics in the later part of the Fifties.

In addition to a catalogue of rich, inventive lyrics, Berry's dozen or so classic recordings offered the world a legacy of R&B-influenced guitar motifs. These guitar stylings were as much a definition of rock and roll as were his simple harmonic progressions and speeded-up 4/4 time.

Wilson alluded to his Chuck Berry debt in 1981, when, looking back, he said "Surfing music at that time wasn't really anything but your Chuck Berry guitar with your Brian, Dennis, Carl, and Michael harmonizing their vocal chords—a good family blend." In that typically modest pronouncement, Brian failed to mention a few other things. While employing Chuck Berry ideas, Wilson had made his own substantial contributions, equaling Berry's work in terms of innovation and artistic depth, even in the early days of 1963.

Rock and roll was more rhythm than blues, and "Sweet Little Sixteen" was a perfect example. Berry devised lyrics reflecting a more optimistic pop culture, and he used faster rhythm, which demanded that one dance. Wilson showed genius in using what was best in Berry's music and adding what was best about the Beach Boys.

Berry's recording of "Sweet Little Sixteen" contains four crucial elements: (1) his classic rhythm guitar chops, (2) a constant cymbal, (3) crude bass arpeggios, and (4) drum and piano embellishment. Outside the bass lines, none of those elements serves to define tonal concepts. Indeed, Chuck Berry music is almost atonal, even as one considers the easy I-IV-V changes and limited vocal range. Berry's music is instead a celebration of rhythm.

In "Surfin' U.S.A.," Wilson took that rhythmic concern and added rich tonal concepts. As has been said too often, he "added harmony." In 1963, Brian kept the guitar, electrified the bass, dropped the piano and cymbal, and added the Beach Boys' voices in their place.

Although the Beach Boys backgrounds in "Surfin' U.S.A." were unsurprising Four Freshmen chords devoid of counterpoint, they were completely refreshing in 1963. Most importantly, Beach Boy harmony contained the unique synergism based upon genetically related voices, what Brian called the "family blend." Many of the more successful vocal harmony groups have been family affairs: the Mills Brothers, the Everly Brothers, the Bee Gees, the Beach Boys. In these groups similar voices with slight (only slight) differences create a kind of two-level harmony involving (1) subtle differences in tone and (2) subtle differences in other nuances, such as natural dynamics. And this cannot be duplicated.

One's local rock group disappoints in attempting to sing a Beach Boys song, because the voices are too disparate. On the other hand, a single voice, overdubbed, will also produce an unsatisfying harmony. An example is the version of "Wouldn't It Be Nice" that Brian completed by himself when the Beach Boys were touring in 1966. He sang all the parts, resulting in a harmony that lacked resonance.

Wilson's addition of background harmony in "Surfin' U.S.A." improved the tonal facts in an obvious way, yet he also made changes in the melody. In "Sweet Little Sixteen," Berry's vocal is highly melismatic. As in jazz singing, energy derives from the manner in which the vocal melody strays from the tonal root. Berry's limited vocal range demanded that kind of melody. In "Surfin' U.S.A." the lead vocals of Mike Love ("If everybody had an ocean...") and Brian Wilson ("Everybody's gone surfin'...") are much more lyrical in both the natures of the

> Chuck Berry's music helped shape, to some degree, Wilson's concept of what his own popular music should be.

sounds and in the actual notes sung. Compare Wilson's "Everybody's gone surfin'..." with Berry's "All the cats wanna dance with..." Brian's two-octave leap to falsetto can be considered a rewrite of the melody, and changes radically the spirit of the song.

Let's move on to production. In England in 1963, the Beatles, like the Beach Boys, forged a new musical style based on rock and roll rhythms. Brian Wilson and the Beatles shared an appreciation for Chuck Berry's rhythmic sensibility, yet, in creating their own records, both moved to a stronger, heavier drum sound. As a side note, one difference between Wilson's early rock and roll sound and that of the Beatles lay

87

in a production concern: the Beatles augmented Berry's cymbal, while Wilson dropped it. Compare the Beatles' "Rock And Roll Music" with the Beach Boys' "Surfin' U.S.A."

In the backing track for the verses of "Sweet Little Sixteen," Berry's signature rhythm guitar stands out, although in a modest way. The simplicity of his entire production reflects the values of an earlier era, when lush harmonies and complex instrumentation were eschewed necessarily.

By 1963, recording techniques and record-pressing quality had improved greatly, to such an extent that Phil Spector could realize his dream of a wall of sound. Brian was too inexperienced to be messing with a wall of sound in 1963. It was enough that the rhythm track of "Surfin' U.S.A." exhibited imaginative improvements over his first rock and roll semi-hit, "Surfin'." Brian did not begin to emulate Spector's wall of sound until 1964, and "Fun, Fun, Fun" was an example of attempts to do so.

"Surfin' U.S.A." had been a hybrid of Berry rhythms and Beach Boy harmonics. "Fun, Fun, Fun" was influenced as much by Spector as by Berry, and it offered a synthesis of sounds rather than a hybrid of styles. There in the first measure behind the lead guitar is the carefully orchestrated percussive assault. Mixed expertly, the drums, guitar, bass, and sleigh bells coalesce into a whole—a new sound that resonates and fires the imagination. It is a heady mix, and it is what Spector did first. Brian had taken little time to master it.

> Brian Wilson and The Beatles shared an appreciation for Chuck Berry's rhythmic sensibility, yet both moved to a stronger, heavier drum sound.

With the wall of sound you don't hear each instrument but rather the larger result of mixed instruments. This is production as an art. In "Fun, Fun, Fun," even the guitar and organ lines in the break lose their individual personalities, coming together in a unique result. Compare that with the break in "Surfin' U.S.A.," which also involves organ and guitar. In that earlier track the organ is very much an organ, the guitar very much a guitar. As if a young artist was just learning how to put colors together.

88

Although Spector's influence on Wilson has been cited many times, two ideas should be added: (1) the speed with which Brian mastered Spector's approach ("Fun, Fun, Fun" was made in January 1964, seven months after "Da Doo Ron Ron" and four months after "Be My Baby") and (2) how Brian moved on from Spector's sound.

By the end of 1964, Brian was producing records that did not simply emulate Spector's wall of sound. In songs like "She Knows Me Too Well" for the *Today* album, he was achieving his own pet sounds—a smooth guitar, a mellow bass—while maintaining Spector's philosophy of the importance of the overall sound.

Compared to "Surfin' U.S.A.," "Fun, Fun, Fun" reveals more movement in the harmonies and a greater sense of voices as instruments. At the end of the latter, Brian lets go with a soaring falsetto, which would become one of the more famous vocal tropes in popular music—up there with Frankie Valli's "Walk Like a Man." In the single version of "Fun, Fun, Fun," that falsetto tag repeats for a good long time (not so in the album version). Like the ending of a Beach Boys concert.

In dwelling on "Sweet Little Sixteen," "Surfin' U.S.A.," and "Fun, Fun, Fun," we witness the emergence of art: from a perfect exposition of a genre, to an experimental combination of styles, to a creation surpassing genre and style. From bluesman Chuck Berry to production genius Phil Spector to consummate artist Brian Wilson.

[Note: when "Surfin' U.S.A." was released in 1963, the single label credited Brian Wilson as author. Chuck Berry's publishing company sued the Beach Boys and won. From that point on, all records have credited Chuck Berry as author of "Surfin' U.S.A." One odd result was that, following the legal decision, Berry's record company issued an album that promised "Surfin' U.S.A." on the sleeve—and that contained "Sweet Little Sixteen" within.]

90

their hearts were full of spring ♩ ♩♪♪

four freshmen and five beach boys

By Jeff Bleiel

Much has been written documenting Brian Wilson's status as one of the greatest and most influential composers and producers in the history of 20th century popular music. Less discussed, however, is the fact that Brian Wilson, in his prime, was one of pop's greatest singers.

It's obvious from both words and deeds that Brian's primary influence as a producer was Phil Spector. While it is less easy to pinpoint one songwriter as being the principal influence on Brian's writing, the names of George Gershwin and Chuck Berry must be near, if not at, the top of the list.

But who was Brian's primary role model as a singer? A convincing case can be made that the answer to this question is, unlike Spector, Berry or Gershwin, not a revered or household name. In fact, it may be a name that escapes even hard-core Beach Boys aficionados – Bob Flanigan.

Bob Flanigan was the lead singer, the "top voice," of the Four Freshmen. That vocal group's influence on Wilson, self-evident upon hearing the Beach Boys harmony, is well-documented in stories about Brian's formative years.

As a teenager, Brian's musical "firsts" were all tied to the Four Freshmen. The first song he remembers being impacted by was their 1955 hit "Day By Day." The first album he ever bought (or rather, begged his mother Audree to buy for him) was, depending on the story, either *Freshmen Favorites* or *Four Freshmen And Five Trombones* (both 1956 releases). And the first concert Brian ever attended was a Los Angeles area performance by the Four Freshmen at the Coconut Grove (although some reports have this event occurring at the Crescendo Ballroom).

All of this, combined with the fact that the Beach Boys eventually performed two songs ("Graduation Day" and "Their Hearts Were Full Of Spring") popularized by the Four Freshmen, makes it clear that Brian Wilson placed the Four Freshmen on a pedestal. But did the admiration become mutual? What does the teacher think of the student?

Bob Flanigan on Brian Wilson: "I hate him because he sings higher than I do."

After providing assurances that he is indeed joking, Flanigan continues: "I'm a great fan of Brian Wilson, his musicianship, and his writing. And since I was the lead singer with the Four Freshmen, I really admire his lead singing."

While aware of their influence on the Beach Boys, the Four Freshmen noticed that Brian Wilson moved his music beyond their parameters. "When they first started, there was an obvious Four Freshmen influence," Flanigan says. "But as Brian wrote more and more, he took the influence we had on him and applied that to what he was thinking. He made the Beach Boys sound like he wanted them to sound, rather than a Four Freshmen copy."

There are a number of similarities and coincidences in the histories of the Four Freshmen and the Beach Boys. Most superficially, both groups achieved their commercial heights while recording for Capitol Records. Both groups' names, alluding to youth, were descriptive of the groups' beginning days, but eventually left them in the position of having to carry on under monikers which they had outgrown. Although known primarily as vocal groups, both the Four Freshmen and the Beach Boys played musical instruments on stage, though their recordings often featured other musicians.

Perhaps most significantly, both groups' vocal blend included the mixture of brothers, cousins and friends. In the case of the Four Freshmen, the core was brothers Don and Ross Barbour and their cousin, Bob Flanigan. (The fourth member of the original group was Hal Kratzsch; by the time Brian bought their records, Kratzsch had been replaced by Ken Errair, who was then replaced by Ken Albers.)

"With the Freshmen, the Barbour Brothers set the 'unison' sound in the group because they both had the same timbre in their voices," Flanigan explains. "I had a similar timbre, but not quite the same. I never had a vibrato, so that's why we never used it." (Likewise, the Beach Boys use very little vibrato.)

While noting that the Beach Boys "voiced things differently" than the Freshmen, Flanigan points out the differences between the "top" or high harmony voices in the two groups.

"Brian sings a lot higher than I do," he said. "The highest note that I could hit comfortably was about a C. I imagine that Brian could sing the E-flat above that, or the F above that very comfortably. But we had pretty much the same sound, and the same approach to lead singing. His intonation was really marvelous. Better than mine, I think."

The Four Freshmen are generally acknowledged as the first group to put the lead voice at the top of the chord, as opposed to the middle of the chord. While they were categorized as a "close harmony" group, they referred to their style as "open harmony" because they spread their voices over the area that a five-part group would cover. With four voices, they sounded like they were singing five-part harmony.

Their biggest chart single was "Graduation Day," which reached number 17 on the *Billboard* chart in 1956. Sharing the airwaves with some early rock'n'roll and R&B vocal group hits, the song obviously connected with 14-year old Brian Wilson. Eight years later, the Beach Boys would memorably perform it (with a touch of comic irony) on their *Beach Boys Concert* LP.

Though the Four Freshmen's arrangement of "Graduation Day" featured an electric guitar (in the jazz vein), it also included a more old-fashioned (i.e. pre-rock) horn chart and a more mannered vocal ("seen-yore prom"). The Beach Boys successfully adapted it into the guitar-bass-drum idiom, and colloquialized the reading of the lyric. (A fantastic and more "serious" studio version, recorded in 1965, was released on the 1990 combined CD reissue of *Today* and *Summer Days*.)

The second song common to both groups' repertoires, "Their Hearts Were Full Of Spring," was featured on the Four Freshmen's *The Freshman Year* LP of 1961. The Beach Boys recorded it (a capella) for their 1962 demo for Capitol Records (this version was released on the 1993 *Good Vibrations* box set), and then lyrically re-worked it into "A Young

Man Is Gone" on the *Little Deuce Coupe* album. Carl, Mike, Al and Bruce sang the original lyric (again a capella) on the *Beach Boys '69/Live In London* album.

On stage in the late '60s, the Four Freshmen performed a comedy bit which had Flanigan attempting to hit the high notes in "Surfer Girl" during a mock audition for the Beach Boys. But on record, the group never brought the Beach Boys influence full circle. Long after their chart heyday and Capitol tenure was over, the Four Freshmen undertook a brief flirtation with the contemporary pop-rock scene in a series of albums on Liberty Records. Though they took cracks at songs by writers such as Paul Simon, Lennon & McCartney, Tim Hardin, and Jimmy Webb, they missed the natural hook of recording a Brian Wilson/Beach Boys song. While their '50s recordings provide a blueprint of where the Beach Boys might have gone had they decided to tackle more pre-rock "standards," the Freshmen's late '60s albums find them content to work in the style of lesser post-Beach Boys pop vocal groups such as The Fifth Dimension and The Happenings.

The legacy of the Four Freshmen will be forever tied to their influence on the Beach Boys. History books and documentaries, which otherwise would tend to ignore the Four Freshmen on their own merits, mention them as part of the Beach Boys "pre-history." While this may be slightly unfair (after all, they were both popular and musically inventive, and they received their fair share of critical accolades, particularly from jazz publications such as *Downbeat*), it does grant them an ongoing recognition, which escapes many other performers of their style and era. For one, Bob Flanigan is quite comfortable with his group's historical connection to the Beach Boys.

"The Beach Boys have always said nice things about the Four Freshmen, which is not necessary at all, and I have a lot of respect for them," Flanigan says. "If we've influenced anything that they have done, that's the greatest form of flattery that you can possibly have in this business. It's something that all the guys are very proud of."

harmony
(don't worry baby)

By Don Cunningham

(Originally published in March 1984)

So often it is said that the Beach Boys are famous for their strong harmonies and that they became successful for juxtaposing a Four Freshmen harmonic style with the rhythmic ideas of Chuck Berry. Less often do we find an analysis of how that harmony is put together. We sing the praises of what is perhaps a national treasure, Beach Boy harmony, and we recognize it in an instant—in the opening bars of a Beach Boy song coming from a radio or adorning an original tune by Chicago, Lindsey Buckingham, Culture Club, or whomever. Yet few have taken time to disassemble Beach Boy harmony to see what is there.

I would like to take a moment to peek inside the famous harmony and perhaps create a better understanding and appreciation of the legacy. I will concentrate on the first eight measures of "Don't Worry Baby" to consider what is possibly an archetypal Brian Wilson harmony. That harmony is also present in slightly altered form behind the first eight measures of the second and third verses of the recording.

Prior to 1964's "Don't Worry Baby" Brian Wilson had produced stunning examples of Beach Boy harmony, from "Surfer Girl" to the *Little Deuce Coupe* album, and after "Don't Worry Baby" would come years of imaginative, memorable harmonies. I choose to look at these particular measures not only because they manage to convey what is good about Beach Boy singing, but also because "Don't Worry Baby" expresses a post-Four Freshmen approach to harmonic structure and movement.

Early 1964 and the arranging of "Don't Worry Baby" found Wilson at ease, structuring harmonies using his own creative impulses, the Four Freshmen approach having been totally absorbed. The vocal arrange-

95

ment in the introduction of "Don't Worry Baby" appears, at first glance, to be simpler than arrangements in many Four Freshmen and early Beach Boys recordings. That is because Brian was beginning to step away from the lush, earlier formulas, learning to economize, and daring to be creative. Although "Don't Worry Baby" was no leap to experimental form, it was a significant advance. It stands midway between "Surfer Girl" and "Heroes and Villains," and therefore is a good choice to represent his canon.

During the first eight measures, the notes in the lower staff are played by a bass guitar, plucked in such a way that the sounds do not quite coalesce with the vocal harmony above. The bass E represents the only tonic note in the chord of the first measure (at least to my ears). Apparently no voice in the upper staff adds the tonic E to Dennis' G-sharp and Alan's B (the major chord would be E-G-sharp-B)—although Mike is possibly singing E weakly. Whether Mike is hitting an E or singing G-sharp along with Dennis, the point is made that Mike does not sing a bass part. His voice is a low tenor, in this case a full octave above the bass E. Indeed, Beach Boy harmony does not employ a bass vocal part, as does the harmony of, for example, country-western vocal groups. The Statler Brothers are a good example. The use of a deep bass voice by such groups localizes their sound.

> Others fail to duplicate Beach Boy harmony because it is characterized more by those five voices than by a particular arrangement.

That first chord is dense, even though few notes are represented. The density is due to the closeness of Alan's and Dennis' notes and the fact that they are joined by others (Carl and Brian hitting Alan's note? Mike hitting Dennis' note?). There is, importantly, a concentration of voices in the middle of the upper staff, and they are joined not by a lower bass voice, but by Brian's pure strong falsetto-B an octave above Alan (and Brian himself?). Here is Beach Boy harmony, characterized not so much by the spreading of similar voices as by the concentration on a few close notes of uniquely compatible voices: Mike's nasal low tenor; Dennis' breathy mid-range; Carl's more delicate mid-range; and (to quote Carl) Alan's "bright timbre" higher up and Brian's "very complete" falsetto-soprano.

Others fail to duplicate Beach Boy harmony because it is characterized more by those five voices than by a particular arrangement. However, the arrangements must not be discounted, especially when they involve counterpoint, which also distinguishes Beach Boy harmony from that of others. The second measure of "Don't Worry Baby" contains a modest case of harmonic counterpoint. Alan and Brian rise up to E, separating from Carl, who maintains B, and because of the strength of Alan's "bright timbre" and Brian's "complete" sonority one senses a satisfactory shift within the harmony. Actually, in moving up to the high E, above Dennis and Carl, Alan and Brian create a classical inversion of the E chord.

The related harmonies found in the second and third verses of "Don't Worry Baby" involve more counterpoint. Listen and you will hear Brian's voice moving artfully through the progression—in addition to carrying the lead melody above (thanks to multi-tracking). In the years following "Don't Worry Baby" Brian became increasingly adept at arranging contrapuntal voices, not only in a strictly harmonic sense ("Our Prayer"), but also in a rhythmic sense ("God Only Knows," "Heroes and Villains"). The use of counterpoint separates Beach Boy harmony from harmonies found in folk music. It was rare for folk rock harmony groups such as Crosby, Stills & Nash or America to offer much more than a parallel motion of voices imitating a melody or stating a chord progression. In addition, such parallel harmonies tended to lie above the melodic line, as opposed to Beach Boy harmony, which often would lie underneath the melody. It was the Beach Boys' use of counterpoint that Brian referred to when he spoke of their doing "a Bach thing."

In the second measure, Brian also holds the high falsetto B while the chord inversion occurs below him. This yields a sense of Brian's falsetto as a lead voice, even while acting as an important part of the harmony. I mentioned that Brian's part becomes more contrapuntal in the verses; it should also be noted that in those cases, this background semi-lead is involved in an additional special counterpoint with his prominent lead vocal, which carries the melody. The man did so much.

97

Brian Wilson's falsetto singing is not as exaggerated (as false) as that of Frankie Valli or Lou Christie. Brian's falsetto seems to lie somewhere between the extreme of a Frankie Valli and a normal soprano voice. The sound of Culture Club demonstrates the result of using a more fully soprano voice at the top of the harmony.

In the third measure of "Don't Worry Baby," each voice shifts down to create an A chord. It is another inversion, with Dennis and Mike moving down to E. I am guessing that Carl is singing A just above them, but frankly, I don't hear him. This could be due to Brian's formidable A one octave above and the bass A one octave below. What is interesting about measures three and four, besides the opting for an inversion, is the fact that a suspension takes place. Instead of progressing I-I-IV-V followed by an authentic cadence back to E (I) in the fifth measure, Brian decided to hold the A chord (IV) into the fourth measure. He only does this in the introduction, however. In the harmony of the later verses, the progression goes to B (V) in the fourth measure. In all cases the bass guitar progresses to B.

As mentioned, in the verses Brian's voice is in counterpoint with itself. This reminds me again of the beauty and power in his voice. Surely he had an expert estimate of his own talents, and I often think how he must have been tempted to do it all himself, knowing he could hit a note better than Mike or Alan, knowing his voice was stronger than the voices of Carl and Dennis. But there were two reasons why he didn't do it alone. The first is emotional: Brian always seemed to revel in the notion of the group and cared that the others felt included. The second reason is practical: although Brian had more vocal talent and could reasonably imitate the others' voices, he could not do so 100 percent. He must have realized that the mix of real voices—all five—produced the signature Beach Boy harmony.

It is worth taking out *The Beach Boys In Concert* album on Reprise to witness some interesting variations on the original harmony of "Don't Worry Baby." Alan and Carl share the lead vocal of this mid-1970s live version; the arrangement is again in the key of E. Not surprisingly, Alan's original line in the harmonic plot is absent, even in the introduction, before he takes the lead. Instead there is a higher part, featuring Carl, which fits between Alan's original line and Brian's original falsetto line.

Brian's falsetto part also is missing. The new high part (Carl) begins on high E and is joined by a strong low E, neither a part of the original harmony. In other words, this opening chord is more straightforward than is that of the original. But the second measure in the live version displays more movement. The result is a harmony that, although thinner, still sounds fresh and imaginative. This points again to the fact that the unique mixture of voices makes Beach Boy harmony so satisfying and memorable—that more than the arrangements.

The harmony found in 1964's "Don't Worry Baby" remained derivative of the Four Freshmen, retaining the best aspects of their approach—multiple voices and slight counterpoint. At the same time it incorporated important, if subtle, new ideas. Brian removed certain notes in the chords and concentrated the voices. He toyed with harmonic progression, employing a suspension. He would continue such trends into the late 1960s, eventually focusing more on the

> Why did Brian choose those notes? Why did Bach choose his notes?

choices of a few notes in counterpoint rather than on the presence of many voices as a lush chord. In an economical way, he created marvelous art. Yet if Brian Wilson's Beach Boy harmony never evolved beyond structures similar to those of "Don't Worry Baby," his legacy would be as strong.

To sum up, four major ingredients characterize Beach Boy harmony: (1) three or more voices densely arranged, (2) the strong, unique falsetto of Brian Wilson, (3) counterpoint, and (4) the blend of family-related voices. By considering these factors, one may point to causes for failure of recent songs.

Ingredients 2 and 3 have been most sorely missed in the later years. Brian has been a part-time Beach Boy since 1970 (except for 1976-1977), and the absence of his once-pervasive vocal parts has proved at times to be insurmountable. The absence of a progressive use of counterpoint has hurt equally and has occurred even in songs written by Brian. For years he has demonstrated an inability to complete songs. He has written melodies that cry out for contrapuntal accompaniment ("Good Timin'," "Goin'

On," "Stevie"), yet the songs remain unfinished and unreleased ("Stevie") or released but unimaginatively produced ("Goin' On").

Although one can learn much by doing it, looking at the individual notes in the harmony, as I have done here, provides only a limited explanation. Why did Brian choose those notes? Why did Bach choose his notes? Ultimately we have to listen to the music to learn why. Repeated listenings to "Don't Worry Baby" prove that its values are lasting. Today it sounds as fresh as it sounded in 1964. The same can be said of any great Bach piece. That is why they chose those notes. The great artists choose the right notes, the right colors, the right movements, based on an instinctual understanding. The result is classicism defined by timeless value and enduring strength.

album review: carl wilson

By Paul Kriksciun

(Originally published in March 1981)

Released as part of CBS Records' "Developing Artists" series, Carl Wilson's first solo album is the initial step in what could be an exciting new path for his talents. The album is not without problems, and these will be discussed, but the stronger points in this project seem to be a clear affirmation of Carl's substantial creative role in America's most visionary and influential group, the Beach Boys. Not unpredictably, it is when the ties to Carl's artistic foundation are most pronounced that this project has its greatest success.

Although Carl wrote all the music, this is not strictly a solo venture. His collaborators are Sweet Inspirations member Myrna Smith (backing vocals, all lyrics), and record company executive and long-time Beach Boys fan James William Guercio (bass, production). Smith's lyrics are competent, if not always inspired, and Guercio's bass work is the same. Guercio's production, on the other hand, is somewhat intriguing. In contrast to the classic "wall of sound" techniques, Guercio has chosen a sparser frame for Carl's efforts. Because the production is so simple and closely pared, both the strengths and the weaknesses of the album are obvious.

The album does not get off to a strong start. "Hold Me" and "Bright Lights," the first two tracks, suffer from a distressing similarity in approach. The concept of chord progression is very weak in both cases. The drums (James Stroud) and bass (Guercio) have the soggy, mechanical, "El-Lay" sound so common to the recordings of Linda Ronstadt, James Taylor and Jackson Browne. The vocal interplay between Wilson and Smith breaks no new ground, the rhythm guitar is unexciting, and John Daly's slide guitar is both superfluous and bland. This is unexceptional stuff.

It is not until the third cut, "What You Gonna Do About Me?," that Carl's musical heritage begins to reveal itself. He contributes a beautifully

simple organ on the chorus and utilizes that classic "California Girls" keyboard sound in a fascinating counterpoint with the bass and synthesizer at the bridge. Unfortunately, the vocals are again nothing more than competent.

"The Right Lane," the final track on side one, is propelled by a more powerful rhythm section of Gerald Johnson (ex-Sweet Inspirations, Steve Miller, Dave Mason) on bass and Alan Krigger on drums and syn-drome. Carl's vocal is sincere and convincing in this song of harsh self-examination. "I've been livin' in the right lane, seein' others cruise on by," Carl sings, ultimately pondering "Am I the kind who could run over my brother just to get where I should be?" An effective statement.

Side two is a success. Starting off gently with "Hurry Love," we see much of Carl's talent revealed. This ballad is tender and evocative. Carl's voice is beautiful and as moving as it has ever been. That, friends, is saying something. Backing vocals here caress the meaning of the song in a dream-like web so typical of the Beach Boys.

"Heaven" is another moving ballad. Carl's falsetto is strong and true. His and Myrna's extensive backing vocals are innovative and do not overwhelm the beauty of the lead vocal. John Daly adds some sweet pedal steel guitar which is remarkably free of country and western conventions. The coda is a classic study in the Beach Boys' counterpoint harmony style, executed strictly by Carl in multiple overdubs.

Although meant to be an indictment of competition in the arts and of the star system in general, "The Grammy" falls flat. The "Greek chorus" effect ("We thought you wanted to be a star") is stilted and forced. Too much effort, too little result.

"Seems So Long Ago," a longing memory of lost innocence, concludes the album. The lyrics flow gently and sadly. The vocals are wistful. Carl delivers a song that is genuinely touching, but not cloying.

Noted music critic Noel Coppage has stated that one of the Beach Boys' major contributions to American popular music is that they "hit upon the sound of something that wasn't sure it had a sound until they came along." Coppage also noted that they "use the words mainly to point you in the right direction, and the **sound** to do the actual conveying." It is when Carl Wilson appears most in touch with these concepts that his first solo album succeeds. When it deviates, it becomes merely inoffensive. To be sure, this album is only a first step for a developing artist, and it shows much promise. Let's sit back and enjoy it, but let's also expect better things in the future.

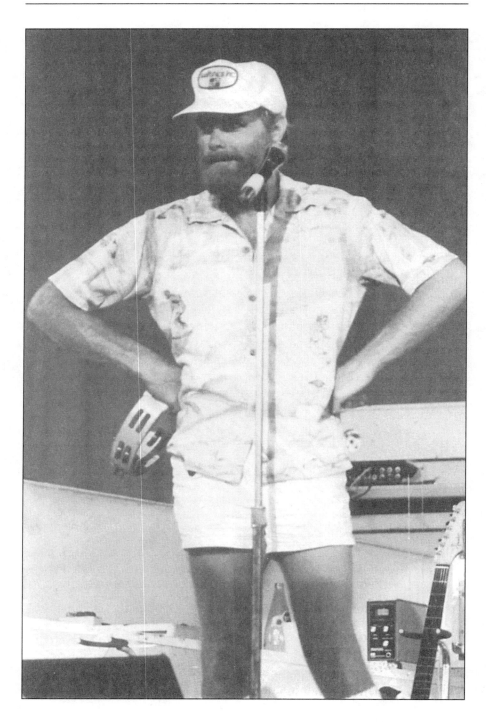

album review: *looking back with love*

By Don Cunningham

(Originally published in February 1982)

One still has to worry about Mike Love. Not about his finances or even his well-being (he's safe with publishing rights and TM), but about his continuing influence over the institution of which he is a 20-percent owner, the Beach Boys. One need only think of his quote from the Dick Clark radio special of last year – "I'm equally as bizarre as Brian ever was...in terms of my scope and my mind" – in order to shudder at sad consequences. At times the most articulate surmiser of the meaning of Brian Wilson and the Beach Boys, he nevertheless has an equal ability to allow his substantial self-possession to lead the group in the wrong direction.

On *Looking Back With Love*, Mike has teamed up with producer and songwriter Jim Studer to create an album that is worse than *First Love*, Mike's unreleased first solo effort. There is no direction to this album, but perhaps that is what Mike wanted. Having taken immense criticism over the years for being the Beach Boys' formula man, always after that marketable "fun in the sun" sound, perhaps he decided to shelve his first album, with its formula sounds, and allow an outside mind to take over.

Some tracks present competent and listenable arrangements, but too many of the songs are totally abysmal. On the positive side, the title track (also the album's first single) is actually a cute rock ditty, although the lyrics are terribly banal. Good, hard drumming propels it, Mike's lead vocal fits the mood, and, of course, the harmony and falsetto are familiar. "Calendar Girl," the Neil Sedaka cat food classic, is a near miss here. A crisp harmony keeps this version alive.

The album's standout is "Teach Me Tonight," although that is perhaps circumstantial. Mike interprets the much-covered Sammy Cahn classic very well, and this track features the album's best production. Percussion is well modulated, the harmony arrangement backs up Mike smartly, and the harmonica break even works.

Then there is the drek. ABBA's "On And On And On," surely a tall task for any cover artist, still demands an apology note to Benny and Bjorn. Someone evidently misread the signs in thinking that the public has been demanding a Caribbean version of the Dave Clark Five's "Over And Over." And Mike's Star Wars version of "Be My Baby" plods along like R2D2 through a swamp, even with all the required percussion.

With the exception of the title track, the four songs written by Studer are extremely docile and forgettable. "Paradise Found," the only song on which Mike receives co-writing credit, is the best of this lot.

In the end, *Looking Back With Love* presents nothing to get excited about. Its greatest value, one hopes, will be in teaching Mike Love a lesson about what is good music and what is not-so-good music.

make it good

the songs of dennis wilson

By Gary Gidman

(Originally published in March 1984)

The emergence of Dennis Wilson as a creative force within (and in later years without) the Beach Boys merits its own chapter in the annals of this longstanding American rock group.

When Brian Wilson went through his years of noninvolvement with the Beach Boys, each of the other band members, at various stages, arose to make his own contribution. While Carl Wilson's activity as producer at the very end of the Sixties is usually cited, it was Dennis Wilson who compared most favorably to Brian in terms of his development as a songwriter, producer, and arranger. Comparisons to Brian are an unavoidable, even necessary, part of the examination of the other Beach Boys' works since Brian's influence was so pervasive, his art so strong. In the case of Dennis' music, the influence of Brian will be seen to be particularly important.

Dennis' outspoken public support for Brian's greatest artworks, *Pet Sounds* and *Smile*, provides evidence that he held the same kind of inspirational awe for Brian's talents as brother Brian reserved for the talents of Phil Spector. Furthermore, it is my opinion that Brian's music laid a groundwork for Dennis' efforts in a way that Spector's music laid a groundwork for Brian's art. In the same way that Brian took Spector's ideas and moved off in his own directions, so Dennis absorbed aspects of Brian's ideas and used them in his own ways.

In a very general sense it appears that Dennis' compositions that were recorded and released by the Beach Boys fall naturally into groups determined primarily by album releases. These begin with the *Friends* album of 1968.

**"Pacific Ocean Blue"-The first solo album
by Dennis Wilson.Next Week.**
On Caribou Records and Tapes

On *Friends*, Dennis collaborated with Carl, Alan, Mike, and others on three songs which were most likely conceived by Brian: "When A Man Needs A Woman," "Friends," and "Be Here In The Morning." The latter is very notable for the use of blocks of alien time signature inserted into the main song structure. Similar, though less prominent, examples of this rhythmic alteration can be found in "When A Man Needs A Woman" and Brian's "Busy Doin' Nothin'." Whether this should be attributed to Brian or Dennis is uncertain; however, the same type of polymetric conceit can be found nowhere else in the Beach Boys catalog except in two other Dennis songs. Either this was an original idea of Dennis', or a quirky idea of Brian's which Dennis liked very much.

Meanwhile on *Friends*, Dennis also debuted two songs cowritten with Steve Kalinich. "Be Still" is a simple idea, almost a chant, and consists only of Dennis singing over an unaccompanied harmonium. It is austere but pleasant, with a rising chord progression leading to a classical-sounding bass suspension.

"Little Bird," the other collaboration with Kalinich, shows a strong measure of Brian's influence, if not his actual hand in production and arrangement, with deftly voiced cello and violins bolstering jazzy harmonies, and martial snare rudiments heralding a memorable vocal tag. The lyric fits snugly into the same homespun "celebration of the mundane" as brother Brian's "Busy Doin' Nothin'." The melody of "Little Bird" is a simple 4/4 scale-based movement with uncharacteristic 3-bar phrases – this on top of some abrupt chord modulations.

1969 saw the release of four more compositions: "Be With Me," "All I Want To Do," "Never Learn Not To Love" (credited solely to Dennis), and "Celebrate The News" (credited to Dennis and Greg Jakobson).

"Never Learn Not To Love" was originally called "Cease To Exist." Charles Manson, who sold the song to Dennis, recorded his own version, which is lyrically very similar to the released Beach Boys version. Musically speaking, the original was a rambling mess. Dennis molded the loose melody, adding a bar of 6/8 time, and a quirky middle-eight. The full-bodied production of "Never Learn Not To Love," featured on the *20/20* album, was crafted by Dennis and Carl. The arrangement employs droning bass, soaring background vocals, steel guitar, and an infectious tambourine-sleigh bell-Indian drum rhythm track which almost steals the show.

"Be With Me" and "All I Want To Do," also from *20/20*, seem to represent the serious and playful sides of Dennis' persona. The former song showed the first signs of the brooding, ballad style which later characterized much of his solo album. It also marked his first attempt to create the expansive timbres showcased in Brian's *Pet Sounds*.

It is certain that Dennis produced both of these songs. I think it is likely that he arranged them both also, at least in part, as the charts seem uncharacteristic of Brian. Building on a chord progression laden with bass suspensions, "Be With Me" features simple, slightly clumsy, blocks of brass. Further, it is propelled by lean, energetic drumming over a combination of piano, baritone sax, and double bass. Where Brian's more progressive arrangements are generally composed around melodic movement (interrelated lines, particularly with regard to the bass), Dennis' "Be With Me"

> Brian's music laid a groundwork for Dennis' efforts in a way that Spector's music laid a groundwork for Brian's art. ♪ ♪

deals in blocked legato chords. What few lines appear are either musically immature (trumpet), or buried in the over-echoed mix (violin and cello, audible in the fade). The background vocals achieve a ragged, improvisational counter which seems a little thin, unlike the ordinary timbre of the Beach Boys. More of these vocal tracks, resembling the raucous interplay of Dixieland jazz, appear throughout the song.

"All I Want To Do" features a brass arrangement similar in complexity to "Be With Me." Stylistically, this song is all-out rock'n'roll: the hard drumming and driving, if unadventurous, bass are in their natural element here. There is a problem with the production, however, as the chorus vocals are inexplicably submerged beneath the brass. Otherwise, "All I Want To Do" is good, clean, musical fun. Well, almost: a close listen to the fade reveals a lot of heavy breathing, grunts and groans, which leave no doubt as to the singer's intent.

110

"Celebrate The News" (the flipside of "Breakaway," the last Beach Boys Capitol single of the Sixties) showed Dennis gaining confidence as an arranger and producer. In the opening melody, Dennis bounces a trendy, oblique lyric over a crude, steady string of eighth notes. This singsong approach to melody is one Dennis seemed to favor from time to time. It would appear again.

The compositional content of "Celebrate The News" is overshadowed by its presentation. The instrumental mix develops into near anarchy: an argument between snare drum and tambourine is overpowered by tympani as slide guitars whine and piccolos trill and squeal. The vocal arrangement is nearly as cacophonous, but occasionally Brian's influence appears (the cascading "ooh"s in the verses, the "whoop-ah"s in the tag). Still, the song abounds with barely organized counterpoint, parts

> **After Brian, it was Dennis who created the most fiercely original and independent musical identity.**

seemingly at odds with each other, teetering on the edge of dissonance. The effect is one of too many ideas spilling over, of a person's curiosity moving a few steps ahead of his judgment.

In the following year, 1970, Dennis' activity reached a peak, when the *Sunflower* album featured four of his songs. Each *Sunflower* song benefited from a production involving all the Beach Boys, especially Brian, as well as the engineering skills of Steve Desper. On *Sunflower*, Dennis apparently yielded control of his songs, just as the other individuals yielded theirs, and as a result, all songs are rendered in grand Beach Boys style.

"Slip On Through" commences with another singsong melody which eventually matures over a percolating rhythm track consisting of congas, synthesizers, and brass. The background vocals are everywhere, snaking through the verses and nearly upstaging Dennis' impassioned vocal in the choruses – where one or more Honeys augment the group.

"Got To Know The Woman" seems to parody the previous album's "All I Want To Do." Here, two dueling boogie-woogie pianos, along

111

with vocals by the Honeys, replace the brass section of the earlier song. Dennis' self-effacing vocals, along with the group's humorous doo-wop chorus lines, serve notice that the intentions here are all in fun.

"It's About Time" (written by Dennis, Alan, and Bob Burchman) may have started out as a jam session. The song's introduction, a simple monophonic riff, repeated over driving drums and congas, seems to imply such an origin. The forgettable lyric delves once again into the themes of self-discovery. In general, "It's About Time" appears undeveloped in contrast to the rest of *Sunflower.*

The same cannot be said of "Forever." Written by Dennis and Greg Jakobson, "Forever" is widely regarded as one of Dennis' best songs. Its haunting melody, delivered with soulful restraint by Dennis, unfolds over acoustic guitars, lap steel guitar, and the tick-tocking tambourine and snare idea used in "Celebrate The News." Subdued group vocals give way first to crescendos bolstered by tympani, and finally to a powerful chorale during which Brian (who can be heard throughout the song echoing the melody with a sympathetic descant of nonsense syllables) improvises brilliant vocal counterpoint. Organ and vibraphone surface to color the fade.

Apparently from the same *Sunflower* recording sessions came "San Miguel," another Dennis Wilson-Greg Jakobson effort, which remained unreleased until 1981. A charming, upbeat number sung by Carl, this track features castanets, marimbas, a stirring trumpet cadenza, and strong vocals from the whole group.

In the same year that those five songs were completed, Dennis also released a solo single in England ("Sound Of Free" / "Lady"). Assisting Dennis on this project was Daryl Dragon (a.k.a. "Rumbo"), who later gained fame as one-half of The Captain and Tennille. The son of a renowned conductor, and himself an accomplished musician, Dragon's involvement with "Sound Of Free" must be deemed slight, as it is a very rough and poorly realized recording, even when compared to Dennis' first efforts. Over a muddy brew of layered keyboards, guitars, saxophones, and barely audible drums, Dennis renders a tentative melody, and shows the first signs of the strain which would dominate his vocal performances thereafter. In addition, background vocals are nominal, perhaps due to an attempt to disassociate from the group's image (even though the lyric is by Mike Love).

"Lady" features no background vocals, but benefits from a much cleaner production and a Daryl Dragon string arrangement. This melody is of the same aesthetic caliber as "Forever," though more melancholy, and somewhat at odds with the lightly percussive rhythm track. "Lady" was later recorded by Spring (as "Fallin' In Love").

No more of Dennis' material surfaced until 1972 and the *Carl and the Passions — So Tough* album, although he was writing and recording material throughout 1971. Apparently his two offerings on *So Tough* were of some vintage. "Make It Good" and "Cuddle Up," both cowritten with Daryl Dragon, feature full orchestral string sections over a grand piano. "Make It Good" is an enigmatic piece, built around a seemingly endless series of chord changes, resulting in a shifting tonality akin to Brian's "This Whole World." However, while that song compressed the changes into a circular, resolved form, repeated throughout the arrangement, Dennis' song contains no structural repetition at all – it never returns to a starting point.

> "Love Surrounds Me" is perhaps the darkest piece in Dennis' catalog, reflecting the sad state of his outlook at the time.

Nevertheless, the musical structure is very powerful, served well by skillful arranging of both strings and brass (which enters to push the vocal higher, toward the climax and fade). Rolling tympani, submerged in the mix, sustain a feeling of movement across legato sections and accent numerous crescendos. While the melody feels a little rough, possibly improvised over the finished instrumental track, the vocal delivery is intense, and the emotional power which drips from this track is impressive and undeniable.

"Cuddle Up" is similar in arrangement and more conventional in form. The verse melody and chord progression could be a variation of "Forever," leading to a memorable chorus which uses the same loose, competitive vocal backing that distinguished "Be With Me" and "Celebrate The News." A lovely piano interlude introduces a wordlessly sung verse, after which the song reaches its powerful conclusion. Instrumentation differs from "Make It Good" only inasmuch as electric bass is used. Production on both songs is clean, though the use of artificial echo on the chorus vocals of "Cuddle Up" seems out of place in the orchestral setting.

113

Dennis brought two songs to the 1973 *Holland* album, "Steamboat" (lyric by Jack Rieley) and "Only With You" (lyric by Mike Love). The first, a bouncy, chugging moderato piece, attempts, through various percussive effects, to approximate the sound of a steam engine. Carl sings a verbose, slightly dumb lyric about the "steamboat of living." Organ and upright piano anchor the track, which also features steel and acoustic guitars, electric piano, vibes, bells, jaw harp, and synthesizer. Loose, doodling harmonies come together for the pleasing "oh don't worry" refrain, which closes the track. The jaunty, humorous mood of this song enhances the homespun Americana subtheme of the album, thanks in part to a compromised production by Carl and Dennis – rougher than the group's normal style, and smoother than many of the things Dennis has done.

"Only With You" is a straightforward ballad. Carl sings again, managing to summon a little of Dennis' grit. Production is left to Dennis alone. The echoed piano, bass, and drum are embellished only by vocals and a string quartet, affording an intimate texture, as befits the piece. After the "all I wanna do-om" hook lines, the verse chords are played in 3/4 time to close the song, once again taking liberties with meter. This is a mature piece.

Dennis' solo album *Pacific Ocean Blue,* released in 1977, contained metric quirks ("Moonshine," "Thoughts Of You," "Time"), singsong lapses of melody ("You And I," "Pacific Ocean Blue") and densely voiced orchestration ("End Of The Show"). Curiously, the rough, Dixieland-style of vocal harmony was absent. One can only speculate as to why.

The Beach Boys' *L.A. (Light Album)* of 1979 contained the last two of Dennis' songs recorded and released by the group. "Love Surrounds Me" (written by Dennis and G. Cushing-Murray) is perhaps the darkest piece in Dennis' catalog, reflecting in spirit, if not in lyric, the sad state of his outlook at the time. A typically dense track of layered keyboards and guitars over thin, funk-styled electric bass and terribly inconsistent drumming is made confusing and frustrating by Bruce Johnston's unfocused mix. Banks of echoed group vocals add to the mess. Dennis sounds tired, and seems to be calling out for someone's love to enfold and assure him. In retrospect, I find this song frightening.

"Baby Blue" is a brighter composition, given a more coherent arrangement and a smarter mix. A lean blend of piano and guitar introduces an attractive motif upon which the main theme builds. This is sung by Carl until Dennis takes over when the meter stalls, ushering in brass and strings. Later the guitar reappears, and the ending features a single rack tom in the recapitulation and fade. The group vocals remain strong throughout "Baby Blue." The arrangement is credited to Dennis, and while it shows no great stylistic differences from the blocked legato approach of the earlier "Be With Me," it is more knowing, more in synch with the rhythm track and the lead vocal.

Especially in terms of songwriting, Dennis Wilson's passing leaves a significant gap in the ranks of the Beach Boys. After Brian, it was Dennis who created the most fiercely original and independent musical identity, exploring areas of style, texture, and influence largely foreign to, or discarded by, the group. The prolific nature of Dennis' creativity drove him to work outside the group long before Carl or Mike. His love for rough, boisterous textures and production values seems totally at odds with the body of Brian's work through *Sunflower*. Yet nothing Dennis ever did was so far removed from the Beach Boys canon that it couldn't, with certain added production values and vocal arrangements, be brought into the group concept.

The fact that Dennis could absorb and utilize so many subtle aspects of Brian Wilson's songwriting style and instrumental arranging techniques is as good a measure of his talent as is anything else. Beyond that, Dennis made his own brave imprint on the songs he wrote and produced. So far, his efforts have proven to be second, in inspiration and worth, only to the art of brother Brian.

brian wilson, class clown

By Don Cunningham

(Originally published in March 1981)

I recently came across a meaningful segment in the Showtime Beach Boys documentary, which aired in the past year. The group was sitting together and at one point Brian alone was talking away to interviewer Ben Fong-Torres. Brian was going on about his songwriting habits. Suddenly he looked around, realized how serious he had become, and blurted out "It's embarrassing; here I am rapping my head off." The rest of the guys broke up. They knew what Brian had suddenly realized — that he had become too serious with this interviewer, and that was not good for the image. Brian then shouted "I like food... creative food." The others laughed harder. Brian Wilson, class clown.

That is a strong piece of evidence for the Brian-is-normal-and-just-fooling-everybody theory. His intentions were obvious in this case, and his voice and manner were, for a moment, those of Brian Wilson circa 1965. He then went on in an off-handed, joking way, saying he enjoys "arguments...other people's arguments." *Rolling Stone* published the quotes about food and arguments. In that context, they sounded so bizarre—and Brian sounded mentally ill.

This is a good example of how Wilson can manipulate the media, fostering the Brian-is-crazy theory and thereby maintaining a kind of privacy for himself. The interviewer asked him about the single "Goin' On," and Brian shifted into that strategy we've witnessed so many times. Sounding serious and oddly excited (child-like?), he stammered and repeated himself: "Oh, 'Goin' On,' yes, that's the—group's favorite that we've done; it's part of this new album, and everybody's screaming 'single single single.' It's one of those kind of records where we didn't wanna— I mean we just wanted to keep at it and at it and at it until we had it perfect. But we just—it got in our blood. Heh."

passing the baton

the beach boys live, april 5, 1982

By Don Cunningham

(Originally published in August 1982)

Like Las Vegas in sheepskin, the gaudy Chateau de Ville in Framingham, Massachusetts lay with a foxy grin, waiting to consume a portion of the lifeblood of the touring Beach Boys.

It's been some twenty years since the Beach Boys, in their infancy, used to play to such small, gymnasium-sized crowds. Then they would be hoping for bigger audiences. Now they seemed to want the smaller crowd, as if they wished to have the smallest number of witnesses following their decline.

The show was brief, stale, and uninspired. The group ran through a set which had been pared down to the easiest songs. The side show was no better, with Brian shouting hoarsely and like a madman into his microphone, Dennis strutting like a drunk with his arms raised, accepting plaudits for ancient efforts, Mike and Bruce babbling on obliviously, and Alan scolding the audience (but not Brian) for smoking cigarettes.

It was impossible to take my eyes off Brian. Twitching his face, squinting his eyes, and screwing up his mouth, he was higher than Voyager I, peeking over the grand piano that served to hide his swollen, 260-lb. body. At one point, he jumped up, performed a dangerous pirouette, and stuck his huge belly in the direction of the audience. No cheers.

Nevertheless, Mike introduced Brian as the lead on "God Only Knows." The music rose, the lights moved to the piano, and Brian's head tilted sideways and toward the rear of the stage. From his throat emerged a

119

choking "I may not always love you, but long as there are stars ...aaaarghh...rrrrr...aaarrrghhh...stop...stop...Bruce, you sing it. I'm too hoarse."

They began again with Bruce taking up the lead (after suggesting that he and Brian sing it together). But Bruce also quit due to a cold in his throat.

What happened next was dream material. As Bruce's voice faded, the lead was assumed quietly by Jeff Foskett, a recently acquired supporting musician who looks like the currently-absent Carl Wilson. A fantasy emerged: a single spotlight shone on Jeff, who gave it all he had. He became Carl Wilson. No, he became the Beach Boys. He served the wishes of the audience. He took the baton, the energy from the band members who lost their ability to focus on that energy. He moved that focus back to where it belongs – the music. "God Only Knows" came alive, and the strength of the song itself took over, to the immediate pleasure of both the audience and the Beach Boys.

all summer long

By Don Cunningham

(Originally published in September 1979)

Would you believe "All Summer Long" was never released as a single in the United States? This is surprising to anybody who regards it as one of those perfect Beach Boys hits reflecting, for example, the summer of 1964. Perhaps it was not released because of the surplus of other Beach Boys hits at the time. Yet Brian Wilson and Capitol recognized its thematic potential when they named the sixth Beach Boys album *All Summer Long*. That album is one of their best, owing in part to the presence of this song.

In the Sixties, singles were the rule, especially singles that could embody all the ingredients of conceptual development in under 3 minutes. Here was the consummate summer single. Listening to "All Summer Long" one hears more than what is sung: the beginning of summer, lazy afternoons, tireless nights, expectations, surprises, summer's end. Brian developed in his humble way a set of lyrics that evoke the simple pleasures of summer, including spilling Coke on her blouse, wearing thongs, and hearing "our song" now and then. A critic might ask, where is the teenage angst? The answer is that the bummer nights and sunburnt days exist right there, below the surface of "All Summer Long." The song's total commitment to joy reflects an awareness of the negative aspects in the form of the human tendency to remain positive.

Brian Wilson's lyrics have always been honest, speaking through us—whereas Mike Love's lyrics smack of a latest little-gestalt trip and Van Dyke Parks' lyrics, although enjoyable, don't approach a common denominator. Wilson's lyrics have consistently hit on our level, as if springing from within each of us, feeling, searching.

The only song on the *All Summer Long* album with an ABABA structure is the title song. This structural symmetry contributes to the idea that "All Summer Long" is in part a story, a conceptualization of a period: summer. The second B section is partly instrumental, yielding a sense of development.

"All Summer Long" does not qualify as a tonal masterpiece. It involves vocals that are near-misses, harmonies that sound rough-hewn, and a fife leading the instrumental section that is, well, flat. Yet Wilson uses achromatic notes in vocal scales and unconventional chord progressions in key development, making "All Summer Long" an ambitious piece of music. In this period of Brian's career, his composing was underrated. Recall that 1964 was the year the Beatles exploded on the scene in the United States, receiving plaudits for I-IV-V songs such as "I Saw Her Standing There." Brian's experiments went unnoticed.

> "As I'm writing this, Carl, Ron Swallow (our traveling buddy and wardrobe man) and three girls along with Earl Leaf are sitting around the coffee table and singing Beatle songs. But my mind is somewhere else right now..."
>
> — Brian quoted on the back cover of
> *Summer Days (and Summer Nights!!)*

As "All Summer Long" opens, a number of voices, in a unique passage, wander teasingly from an initial C before landing on an unusual rest chord: E-flat. The experience is mildly unsettling but fun, like spilling Coke on her blouse. A strong element of "All Summer Long" is the careful use of upward and downward scales, built around a basic C-F-G plot but with bold movements through minors, sixths, and sevenths. Riding up and down, one gets a sense of the changing emotions of love, affection, and other feelings that fill the summers of youth.

Any uncertainty regarding the theme is answered by a production that exudes pure fun. After the famous xylophone introduction, that unusual instrument can be heard throughout and, along with a pleasant fool-around bass, defines the production sound as light, upbeat. With the addition of Wilson's dense vocal-harmonic wall, the sound maintains its freshness—a result of his talent for mixing sounds.

It is good to note that Brian almost always had to create a backing track on top of which would sit the most sumptuous harmonies in American popular music. If a backing track were too cluttered, disaster might occur upon the addition of vocals. Yet note how sublime his instrumental tracks are nevertheless. Phil Spector's music differs from Wilson's in this aspect. Spector could throw everything into a backing track, knowing that, for the most part, only a single voice would be added afterward. It might even be argued that Brian's instrumental tracks, because of the necessity of their being tonally/texturally arresting—as opposed to dynamically/texturally arresting—stand up better than do Spector's in the long run. I suspect that an album of Spector backing tracks would be rather boring.

And Wilson gave us a gem of an instrumental break in "All Summer Long." Fife, sax, and xylophone vie individually for our attention in the charming interlude, which is unique in its rhythmic and textural result. Evidence for his 1964 move toward a larger use of the studio orchestra comes in the way of those instruments as well as the stronger, faster drumming.

George Lucas used "All Summer Long" as the background music during the fade-out of his film *American Graffiti*. He once explained that it was the perfect song, that he had to use it, even though no matter where you were in '62 (the film's period), you were not listening to "All Summer Long." Knowing the dislocation of this 1964 song, a viewer is provided with an extra dimension of thought. If there is an anthem to the summer of '62, it was conceived in the summer of '64 and became an anthem for every summer. In the same way, the events of *American Graffiti* go beyond 1962 to reflect any adolescent coming-of-age scenario.

> Brian almost always had to create a backing track on top of which would sit the most sumptuous harmonies in American popular music.

welcome back, bruce

By Don Cunningham

(Originally published in March 1979)

There seems to be an effect of all that California sunlight, an effect that slows the artistic/creative process over time. Witness the Eagles, Fleetwood Mac, and others, including the Beach Boys. During such decelerations in production, a personnel change in a group will often occur, resulting in one of two things: aggravating the decline or catalyzing a reverse in the trend and bolstering the creative process. It is with great hope for the latter event that we welcome Bruce Johnston back to fuller-time status with the Beach Boys.

Over the years, Bruce has shown artistic courage and a sizable wherewithal. Before, during, and after his first tenure with the Beach Boys, Bruce displayed patience, modesty, and a willingness to work hard — whether singing on "God Only Knows" or writing for the Hudson Brothers.

This is not to say he can be the cure-all for the Beach Boys today. For that we need the renewed energies of the other Beach Boys, especially the Wilsons. However, Bruce could be a catalyst, encouraging Carl to finish some of his songs, pushing Brian to sing a difficult part. More directly, he could contribute new songs and production know-how to new albums.

To be honest, we demand quite a lot from the Beach Boys. Bruce is in a unique position, standing outside the family politics while being a legitimate member. Let's hope that his influence affects positively one of the few groups in the world that can meet the kinds of demands we make.

album review: keepin' the summer alive

By Michael Bocchini

(Originally Published in June 1980)

Although it is stronger than their previous album *L.A. (Light Album)*, the Beach Boys' *Keepin' The Summer Alive* continues to reveal a group in transition, taking a course that is not straight and true.

Throughout the more vibrant cuts, the group relies on a rough-edged harmony which suits the members' more mature voices and the times in which they are singing. "Goin' On," the album's first single, best exemplifies this direction. In a fine integration of music and lyric, the song continues Brian's motif of love lost but not forgotten. Familiar voices strive to blend into a brave pretense of harmonic normality, while disparate vocal and instrumental elements provide an emotional edge which reveals the harsher reality of "goin' on" after love has ended. Carl's solo cry exposes the basic truth of the drama, while the descending harmonic "Aahhs" which follow him reveal the sadness in the acceptance of that truth.

The rhythm track, with quick cymbals instead of the more usual tambourines or sleigh bells, contributes to the sense of acquired maturity in this emotional drama – moving it forward musically and mirroring the greater experience of the group. "Goin' On" is the most successful synthesis of ideas on *Keepin' The Summer Alive*, and probably the best song.

Carl Wilson and Randy Bachman tackle the same dilemma of lost love in their composition "Livin' With A Heartache." The result does not completely satisfy because of its singsong country sound. But Carl's voice in the middle eight abandons the song's slight country twang and provides a soothing and interesting respite from a repetitive sound that seems interminable.

The Wilson-Bachman collaboration works more successfully in the album's title cut. Carl takes the lead vocal in a song which provides him an opportunity to exhibit a flair for a harder brand of rock. The music is proven, as "Keepin' The Summer Alive" remains for the greater part a reworking of Bachman's BTO hit "Takin' Care Of Business." The song bears the true Beach Boys' signature during the middle eight (Carl's contribution?), as it slows to consider the more contemplative virtues of summer days and nights. For a summer anthem of the '80s, one could not require more.

Whether the Wilson-Bachman collaboration will evolve into something fruitful continues to be a question. "Livin' With A Heartache" and "Keepin' The Summer Alive" sound as if they were written by a Beach Boy and somebody else and do not totally fit the Beach Boy canon as do Brian's collaborations, which, for all their experimentation, remain Beach Boy songs.

If "Keepin' The Summer Alive" represents the Beach Boys' successful venture into white rock, "School Days" returns to the group's sometimes-profitable reworking of '50s black rock. Unfortunately, unlike "Rock And Roll Music," another Chuck Berry standard which the Beach

128

Boys managed to transform into the California sound without destroying the song's integrity, "School Days" leaves a flat, white bread taste. This cut sounds more like a '50s white group cover record.

Oddly enough, the song that most closely resembles the sound of an earlier era, "Some Of Your Love," also rings slightly false. From the sax intro and honky tonk piano to the Mike Love lead (nobody but nobody can say "summer" like Mike) and background vocals, this song is good times, AM radio, here comes the summer, Beach Boys. And that's good. However, the effort here is obviously to recreate. A checklist of Beach Boy techniques has been utilized, with the "Be True To Your School" harmonic progression very transparent. A group cannot cover its own sound, but "Some Of Your Love" comes close to the Beach Boys copying, instead of singing, a Beach Boys sound. And that's not great.

A song that advances the Beach Boys' sound, "Oh Darlin'," utilizes Carl's clear "middle eight" voice and the rough-edged harmony beautifully to produce a fully realized love song. The ecstasy of newfound love is supported by a broad, romantic horn intro, vibrato harmonies, sensual percussion, and heraldic horn phrases. A unique dissonance in the harmony of the middle eight is Brian at his creative best. The roots of *Pet Sounds*, acknowledged in "Oh Darlin'"'s lyrical fade, are evident in theme and music. Brian and Mike show a fine control in this composition, which moves easily through the wonders of love. One wonders what a full Brian Wilson production would have wrought.

> "Sunshine" will not become a classic, but it shows Brian working at his playful experimentation.

Also encouraging is producer Bruce Johnston's inclusion of Brian and Mike's "Sunshine" on this album. "Sunshine" will not become a classic, but it shows Brian working at his playful experimentation. Like sunlight and shadow seen through the leaves of a tree moving in a Caribbean breeze, the sound of steel drums underscore a Jamaican beat. This is Brian at his lighthearted, inconsequential best.

On the other hand, "When Girls Get Together" reveals Brian at his ponderous worst. With "California Feeling," "Its Over Now," and "Still I Dream Of It" still waiting to be included in an album, the choice of this older song, with its dirge-like melody, sexist lyric, and uninspired production, mystifies. The placement of these cuts side by side exposes a production flaw in seeing them as equally worthy of inclusion.

A second jarring juxtaposition occurs at *Keepin' The Summer Alive*'s conclusion. Brian and Al's efforts are successfully realized in "Santa Ana Winds." Backed by classic Western instrumentation (guitar, banjo, and harmonica), the timeless nature of existence finds embodiment in a metaphorically rich lyric. The incessantly strummed guitar and/or banjo invoke the timelessness described in the lyric, and never become boring due to a smart, dynamic blend of other sounds, especially harmonies. Al's lead begins with observation about the wind as it moves to the sea, and his relationship with it. The relationship deepens as Al's lead is transformed from observation to personification. He has become the wind and can offer its benefits to others. The transformation from the aridity of the desert to the fecundity of the sea represents the reconciliation of seeming opposites – whether they be air and sea or man and nature – in an endless harmony.

This message becomes more vivid when seen in relation to Bruce Johnston's "Endless Harmony." A song about the Beach Boys does a disservice to the act of their singing and a listener's experience of it. Johnston pays mediocre homage to his friends in an overly lush, saccharine production which results in mere puffery and an exercise in wasted harmony.

Thus, *Keepin' The Summer Alive* ends on a disappointing note. Hearing the harmonies in "Endless Harmony" is, to mix a metaphor, like looking through the wrong end of a telescope. "Goin' On," "Oh Darlin'" and "Santa Ana Winds," are successful because they carry the hopeful note of expanding talent. "Keepin' The Summer Alive" is an old song strengthened by a touch of Beach Boy magic by Carl. "Sunshine" reminds one of the joys of being playful again a la Brian. "Some Of Your Love" brings back top down weather and high school summers.

With those tracks, *Keepin' The Summer Alive* should have provided the Beach Boys with a commercial success. However, a breakthrough single has not resulted at the time of this review.

What remains on the album prevents it from becoming a unified artistic success. In its totality, *Keepin' The Summer Alive* cannot claim more accolades than it deserves. The album stands as a vehicle for some very interesting and worthwhile material, but misguided song selection and production reveal a group entering its third decade of performing searching for a viable musical course to chart, and rushing into production with mixed results.

While one cannot underestimate the positive contribution of Bruce Johnston's production, especially his therapeutic third-party politics, one cannot deny his culpability in the album's shortcomings. Much of the promise of this album comes from the names Wilson, Jardine, and Love. In the final analysis, the future direction of the Beach Boys rests with them, and should be placed in their hands if the Beach Boys are to prevail.

smile

By Don Cunningham

(Originally published in February 1983)

An eerie soundtrack of fire music made of violins and bass, which is more devilish than cataclysmic; pounding drums and low chants, which are designed to put American Indians in your living room; the repetition of a lyric phrase, which continues for so long that a mild sense of paranoia develops. These are sounds from *Smile*.

A half-dozen or so unreleased tracks from the *Smile* sessions have leaked out and are spreading around on tape. Although these fragments paint only a corner of the picture that would have been *Smile*, they suggest a direction Brian's mind was taking and the large obstacle that faced him in 1967.

With his new music, Wilson was clearly moving out of the art form that had been the basis for his great successes. For years he had incorporated influences of R&B, folk, jazz, and more into pop. The popular song was his milieu, and as he would lay down inspired, unusual musical plots within its confines, he would rely on many of its parameters.

If he used creative harmonics in "The Little Girl I Once Knew"—pushing the limits of pop—he nevertheless was careful to retain the essence of pop and thus beatify his experiments. With his vision, that was a guarantee. With *Smile*, there would have been no such guarantee. And the theories to explain Brian's refusal to finish *Smile* go on and on.

Another theory, a favorite of mine, involves the easy boredom that seemed to be part of Brian's nature. People are amazed when they learn that, in the early days, he would pump out three or four albums in the space of a year. Yet that is how he worked best—rapidly—finishing before he would tire of an album. His most drawn-out project was *Pet*

133

Sounds, yet that album contained studio chatter recognizable during quieter moments. Did boredom set in before Wilson could make a final cleansing/revision of the tracks?

Smile would have been a conceptual album requiring an extended, complex organization—like one long song. Could the man who had just enough patience to complete a 3-minute song sustain an interest in such an extended form?

Perhaps it was not so much that Wilson failed to envision the completed *Smile* project as that the *Smile* project failed to hold his interest. Perhaps his mind moved past the project before it was completed.

Yet the musical impulses on the *Smile* tapes are fascinating. The fact that the Beach Boys' recording company does not force the release of a *Smile* anthology of some sort continues to puzzle me.

ḥeroes and villains

By Don Cunningham

(Originally published in September 1980)

A famous story describes Brian Wilson, in 1967, taking the final mixdown of "Heroes And Villains" to a nearby Los Angeles radio station to offer it for a late-night first-time broadcast. In a gesture symbolic of the creative content of that long-awaited Wilson release, the artist and retinue traveled in a limousine caravan to the radio station, where they were denied admittance. Brian had even considered predominant astrological features in choosing that night—but he was shut down anyway. They say he was crushed.

My feeling has always been that the disc jockey who rebuffed Brian Wilson that night might have managed to bring to a halt the six-year upward spiral of Wilson's artistic achievements. The phenomenal rise had begun with "Surfer Girl" and "Surfin' Safari" and, in 1965-1966, escalated exponentially with *Pet Sounds* and *Smile*. After "Heroes And Villains," the ride was over. In the subsequent years we would be treated to tantalizing but only infrequent new songs ("This Whole World," "'Til I Die") and *Smile* pieces ("Cabinessence," "Surf's Up").

At times Brian's genius would surface, but its scope of implementation would be severely curtailed. Rather than albums that would leap forward in creativity and make a splash in the pop music scene, Brian would create, in humble guise, small works such as an R&B-flavored album suffused with gentle humor (*Wild Honey*), an album filled with close harmonies acting as metaphor for the fruits of simple kindness (*Friends*), and an album in which plodding synthesizers and hard percussion would describe a man smiling through tears (*The Beach Boys Love You*). After "Heroes And Villains," there would be no further attempts to reign as artist supreme in the pop scene.

"Heroes And Villains" did well on the 1967 music charts (#12 nationally), testimony, again, to Wilson's uncanny ability at the time to push the limits of pop while remaining popular. "Heroes And Villains" was the only Beach Boys hit with lyrics not immediately understood by listeners. It was the Beach Boys song with the greatest percentage of nonsense syllables and a surprising amount of a capella singing. It was an abridgment of a larger work which was destined to reside in the *Smile* vault. It was arranged in the key of D-flat.

Who knows what "Heroes And Villains" would have sounded like on *Smile*. Abrupt edits in the released version hint at points of departure, but little else. The version distilled for AM radio play features the following structure: A-A-B-A*-A**-A***-A****-B-fade. The first A sections contain the rapidly sung story line, based in a humorous melodic descent longer than an octave. The progression each time is D-flat-E-flat-A-flat-D-flat. A bridge of minor character shifts into the B section (the "music box" or "bicycle rider" chorus), which features a related plot beginning on E-flat-minor.

The next A sections (1 and 2 stars) contain fewer words. A "la la la" lyric, reminiscent of "na na na" from "Good Vibrations," rambles down the A melody, eventually yielding to vocalized words. The next descent features a capella "doo doo doo"s in counterpoint, which play off the initial A story. After another bridge, the song returns to the first sense with "My children were raised..." and one realizes that Wilson is producing musical plot in a big way by causing the basic refrain to evolve. At first, the nebulous lyrics follow the simplest musical accompaniment. The middle A sections portray an acquiescence of Van Dyke Parks' lyrical ideas to the powerful interplay of sounds in Brian's polyphonic nonsense syllables.

> "Heroes And Villains" was the only Beach Boys hit with lyrics not immediately understood by listeners.

The final time through, lyrics return, but Brian is experimenting with rhythm, so that, if one does not immediately understand "my children were raised" or "I've been in this town," one can glean intent from the slowing tempo—a questioning lament introduced by another bridge of minor character.

An interpretation of Van Dyke Parks' lyrics in "Heroes And Villains" could constitute another essay altogether. Two things come to mind in summing up Parks' work: (1) he gave the song lyrics steeped in allegory and humor, reaching for a meaning that encompasses the American experience (in the same way, perhaps, that the entire *Smile* album would have reached); and (2) his words blended successfully with Wilson's production. In the dream-like and timeless qualities of the gunfight and the comic confidence of the protagonist "fit with the stuff to ride in the rough" Parks makes grand allusion to the contradictory nature of our American character, with precision and economy.

In concert, the Beach Boys sing the so-called "bicycle rider" lyrics ("Bicycle rider, see, see what you've done/to the church of the American Indian") during the chorus in "Heroes And Villains." "Bicycle Rider" sometimes is given credit as being another complete song from *Smile*—either that or it played a role in a longer *Smile* version of "Heroes And Villains."

Although originally featuring Brian on lead vocal, in concert, "Heroes And Villains" has come to be Al Jardine's number, and a good job he does with it. His voice is complex in its geographical allusions—country/urban/eastern/western—so that he lends additional support to the song's referral to the American experience.

Along with "Surf's Up" and "Cabinessence," the abridged "Heroes And Villains" brings to mind the tragedy of the unfulfilled notions of the *Smile* project. If these songs are an indication, *Smile* would have been an artistic adventure in which complexities of sound captured the rich fabric of the history and meaning of America. The country emerged from the eastern shore and has evolved to the point where the cultural vanguard sits on the western shore. We are life that sprang from the ocean, and we will return some day to that watery mass. It would have been entirely appropriate for the *Smile* statement to be made by an author named "The Beach Boys."

california girls
and let him run wild

By Don Cunningham

(Originally published in March 1981)

Two songs from 1965's *Summer Days (And Summer Nights!!)* stand out, each in its own way, as mature triumphs in the career of Brian Wilson. They are "California Girls" and "Let Him Run Wild." In that album, Brian gave us strong evidence of a remarkable depth of creative wherewithal. Tiring of the earlier Beach Boy album formulas and looking toward future concepts and conquests, he threw together a motley but satisfying collection of songs. All by himself. The songs were as texturally interesting as one could wish. "I'm Bugged At My Ol' Man," "Salt Lake City," and "Then I Kissed Her" contributed rich, disparate voices to an album of musical and thematic consensus.

Disregarding the version of "Help Me, Rhonda" (another triumph) placed on this album because of its single success, the songs "California Girls" and "Let Him Run Wild" somehow stand taller than the rest. "Salt Lake City" is wholly enjoyable, but "California Girls" is art fashioned by a genius. "Then I Kissed Her" is a top-drawer textural statement, yet "Let Him Run Wild" went places no one save Brian Wilson dreamed of in 1965.

Once in awhile a song comes along with rare qualities of perfect balance: universal in theme yet personal in outlook; lyrical and singable, even folk-like, yet high art. "California Girls" is such a song—one that kindergarten kids will be learning 20 years from now. It has as much kinship with Woody Guthrie's "This Land Is Your Land" as with "Surfin' U.S.A." It is popular American Folk Music.

"Let Him Run Wild" is more a love song, although very much a Brian Wilson love song, with that man's philosophy and feelings. It is perhaps a culmination of the early period Wilson love songs, which are general

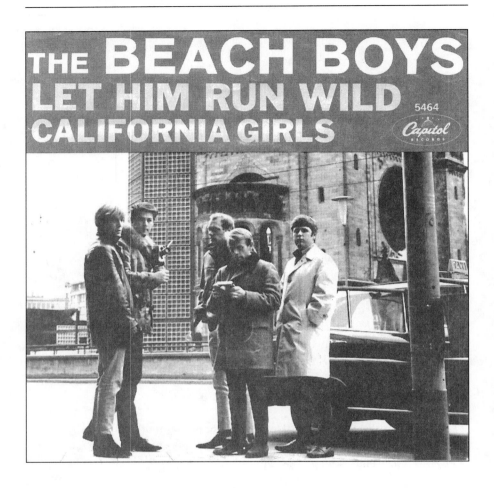

in tone. The person who should run wild is definitely one of thousands of third parties in three-party relationships. With the album *Pet Sounds* in 1966, Wilson moved beyond this to a fully personal love song. Because of that shift, to really understand and love "Don't Talk (Put Your Head on My Shoulder)" it helps to understand and love Brian Wilson. This reminds me of John Lennon's love songs—the early ones with the Beatles yield a general perspective, while his late-Beatles and post-Beatles love songs are more inner-directed. A person could get into a discussion of the artists' alienation from the public. "Let Him Run Wild" and "California Girls" predate that problem.

142

Brian makes a complete musical statement in "California Girls" before the first word is spoken by Mike Love. The introduction is powerfully famous and has been used to open the band's live show for some years now. Permutations of the A-chord, highlighted by horns and drums in a slowed tempo, sum up like a proper overture the song that will follow—while adding depth and meaning to it. The regular song parts are in common time, the structure is ABABB with a I-I7-IV-V7 progression in the verses and a subtle chord plot in the chorus. The sevenths in the verses appear to be important character elements.

More important on the creative level are the instrumentation and production. The rhythmic organ of "California Girls" is one of the best uses of organ in all of rock music. The constant melodic jumps of the bass in counterpoint with the syncopated organ are what you and I and the future kindergarten kids can grab onto.

"California Girls' " rich, echoed percussion reminds me that the instrumental track was recorded at Goldstar Studio, Spector's stomping ground. Chuck Britz, Wilson's engineer, has said that this was the first "big band" sound that Brian created. A combination of Spector-type production and inspired songwriting made for the second chart-topping Beach Boys single.

> "California Girls" has as much kinship with Woody Guthrie's "This Land Is Your Land" as with "Surfin' U.S.A."

What was the B-side to that smash single of the summer of '65? None other than "Let Him Run Wild." This strong B-side presents Brian's beautiful reaching vocal floating among more echoed percussion, more colorful organ, and fantastic looping bass runs. Two things stand out: first, Brian's precious vocal interpreting a difficult yet lyrical melody; second, the exciting urgency of the rhythmic ideas—the way the A sections explode into the B sections; the way so many rhythmic elements make the B sections a percussive symphony.

It is possible to wonder about Brian's feelings concerning the use of Mike Love's voice in the lead vocal of "California Girls," especially in light of Brian's statement that he felt Mike "rushed" that vocal. Gener-

ally there might have been frustration on Brian's part in those days, with the public favoring Love's vocals—limited in tone, rhythm, and texture—more than Brian's stronger leads, with "Let Him Run Wild" being a perfect example.

Musically, "Let Him Run Wild" may be the greater masterpiece. Yet, working as a cultural talisman, "California Girls" looms as the bigger work, operating on a broader level. For the past 20 years, "California Girls" has contributed powerfully to the mythological meaning of California.

Finally, it must be stated that the harmonies in these two songs are the consistently unique, signature sounds of the boys from Hawthorne. Brian's smart, careful arrangements of harmonic parts in both songs are, as usual, further manifestations of his genius. This was what we came to expect in 1965 and what so many wish to hear today.

sunrise: eric carmen

By Gary Gidman

(Originally published in September 1980)

Editor's Note: Throughout the life of the ASM journal, Gary Gidman authored a series of articles called "The Brian Wilson School" which looked at artists whose work displayed a significant influence of Brian Wilson. Many of the artists covered were relatively obscure, but here we excerpt Gary's commentary on the artist he called "America's number one honor student in the Brian Wilson School."

Eric Carmen first came to attention as the principal singer and songwriter for the Raspberries, who scored four Top 40 hits from 1972-1974. Although their power pop sound drew a bit more heavily from the Beatles than the Beach Boys, Carmen contributed tracks such as "Drivin' Around" and "On The Beach" which mimicked the Beach Boys' vocal harmony style and Brian Wilson's production techniques.

The band's fourth and final album, *Starting Over*, included Carmen's two most overt and successful homages, "Cruisin' Music" and "Overnight Sensation (Hit Record)." The latter song has a coda which enters through a transistor radio speaker, surges and dies down to a single piano arpeggio, and then comes crashing back for the fade. The vocal harmonies, while an accurate approximation of Brian's practices, in retrospect were only warm-ups for Carmen's self-titled first solo album.

Eric Carmen, released in 1975, features numerous highlights. "My Girl" sports a refrain that rivals "Marcella" or "Funky Pretty" in the sheer complexity of the vocal counterpoint. "Last Night," with its delightful "dit-dits" in the choruses, takes Brian's "wonder of the mundane" lyric approach ("Busy Doin' Nothin'") and twists it. The verse and bridge lyrics categorically rattle off the day's activities (going to the drugstore,

This slowing down again brings to mind "Good Vibrations," and, as in that song, a ponderous segment yields to a burst of energy. In this case, it is the B section again, which then fades out the song. The minor chords of the fade leave one with a taste of wonder rather than resolution.

The mix of "Heroes And Villains" is cause for frustration to lovers of Brian's instrumental and vocal production techniques. The instruments are pushed back and the vocals, although up front, have an insouciance of their own. They don't jump from the speakers as do the voices of, say, "Don't Worry Baby" or "Keep An Eye On Summer." Magnificent vocal counterpoint is a main character of "Heroes And Villains," yet one is forced to listen hard to hear nuances of that counterpoint. Individual voices refuse to take precedence over each other, yielding to a general vocal character. Each hero and villain gets a line somewhere, but each voice is consumed by the bigger picture of the legacy left by the exploits of those heroes and villains.

> **The mix of "Heroes And Villains" is cause for frustration to lovers of Brian's instrumental and vocal production techniques.**

A track-only version of "Heroes And Villains" would be much appreciated. In it we might hear with greater clarity those sounds Wilson chose to push back in the final mix. The bass parts (guitar and organ) are most evident in the song's opening statement as a driving, pulsating element—life sources of the heroes and villains. Other keyboards become variously evident. I especially enjoy the organ audible at the ends of A sections, which possibly features the famous "empty swimming pool" echo effect. Then there is the unique harpsichord sound in the B sections.

What must be said of the vocals? Perhaps that Brian had come a long way from the Four Freshmen in a few years. His ability to use voices as instruments reached a new peak in "Heroes And Villains." In his use of the sonorities at hand—those untrained Hawthorne voices—Brian was as impressive as Beethoven was using violin, clarinet, and cello. The efficiency and effect of the counterpoint in the B sections is hard to believe. In the A sections, I hear 20 voices, yet at the same time I hear one voice, that of Brian Wilson.

playing some records, reading a magazine), while the chorus acknowledges the wasted time. Here is prima facie evidence that Carmen studied not only the sun'n'fun hits and *Pet Sounds*, but also *Friends*.

With a production featuring sleigh bells and layered vocal harmonies, the pop-rocker "Sunrise" is framed by a symphonic intro and a coda riff paraphrased from Elton John's "Saturday Night's Alright For Fighting." Carmen's sophisticated arrangement of "On Broadway" (the album's only cover) fires the imagination. Is Brian's unreleased version anything like this?

Perhaps the most striking thing about Eric Carmen is the way his compositional style complements his arrangements. Piano is usually the central instrument in the arrangements, and the left hand favors a figured bass employing frequent suspensions (putting a chord against a bass note other than the root pitch, or other than other pitches in the chord), one of Brian's most common practices.

Carmen's second LP, *Boats Against The Current* (1977), continues in much the same vein as its predecessor, but with one difference. The vocal arrangements on the songs "She Did It," "I Think I Found Myself," and the lovely (although mixed down) coda of "Love Is All That Matters" were done, and partially sung, by Beach Boy Bruce Johnston. "She Did It" in particular is a fine recording, probably Carmen's finest tribute to Brian's influence.

His next album, *Change Of Heart* (1978), sees a turn in the road just commencing. Johnston again returns to handle vocal arrangements and backing vocals on the two best tracks, "Someday" (in which the "dit-dits" return to a prominent place) and "Hey Deanie," (which was a huge hit in a cover version by teen idol Shaun Cassidy). The remainder of the album lacks discernable Brian Wilson/Beach Boys influence.

Tonight You're Mine (1980) takes a new musical tack, sort of a more visceral, less sophisticated Billy Joel. Whatever the reasons for this change, the result is our loss.

Carmen is also connected to another project that deserves special mention here — the Euclid Beach Band's self-titled album, which he produced in 1979. This duo from Cleveland, which includes Richard Reising, one-time guitarist in Carmen's band, is stylistically similar to Carmen, though they need improvement in their songwriting. The obvious standout, overshadowing all else on the LP, is the stunning "There's No Surf In Cleveland," a bundle of fun complete with surfing guitars, a modulated solo, "I Get Around" handclaps, and full vocals drowned in echo. A worthwhile addition to any record library, it (even more so than Carmen's own records) conjures the sound and spirit, if not the actual substance, of the Beach Boys.

album review: california u.s.a.

By Gary Gidman

(Originally published in September 1981)

A new Columbia compilation album, *California U.S.A.*, showcases twenty songs by various artists, all owing in some way to the sound or the myth.

Side One commences with a classic. "Summer Means Fun" by Bruce (Johnston) and Terry (Melcher) was released in June 1964, four months after "Fun, Fun, Fun" and one month after "I Get Around." Written by P.F. Sloan and Steve Barri, another L.A. duo whose compositions brought success to the Turtles and Barry McGuire, the song reflects the former song's "fun" attitude, while the arrangement, particularly the complex modulations, structured descents, and bass vocals, owes strongly to the latter. The vocals on this cut are outstanding.

"Girl On The Beach" is a ballad by Rick Henn, formerly of the Sunrays, a California band briefly taken under Murry Wilson's wing after his managerial demise with the Beach Boys. This cut features an interesting melody, smooth harmonies, and a lush, rather conservative sounding instrumental track which makes good use of dynamics and plate reverberation.

Sparks is the musical alias of the Mael brothers, Ron and Russell, two California siblings who found their mid-'70s fame in England after taking up residence there. "Over The Summer," their offering here, is considerably more commercial and Californian in its substance than any other Sparks record this reviewer has ever heard. Sporting a nifty a capella introduction and a simplistic backing track, which reminds one of a television ad for suntan oil, this cut is pleasant fun, though slightly shallow.

A gem of recent origin, "There's No Surf In Cleveland," performed by the Euclid Beach Band under the supervision of Eric Carmen (himself a Brian Wilson School valedictorian), appears next. This is a genuine imitation Beach Boys song, using various lyrical, musical, and production elements of "Surfin' U.S.A.," "I Get Around," and "Fun, Fun, Fun." I enjoy the mock-defiant verse lyrics: "You can go to Philly anytime if the Liberty Bell rings your chimes." Be true to your school.

"Minnesota," by a group called Northern Light, closes the side. The vocals here sound suspiciously like the alleged "Beach Boys" on B.J. Thomas' "Rock And Roll Lullaby." Lyrically, the song is "New York's A Lonely Town" turned around. Musically speaking, the arrangement overshadows the song, with its chugging rhythm section, rack tom substituted for snare drum ("Wild Honey"), and a nice potpourri of instrumental effects, including field recordings of a loon out on some midwestern marsh.

The Inconceivables' "Hamburger Patti" is a riot, with its ridiculous lyric and humorously awkward vocal jump of slightly more than an octave into the falsetto chorus. The arrangement here is aimed at Phil Spector: echo on everything, and a direct quote on bass from "You've Lost That Lovin' Feelin'." Whoever is singing lead here is doing a creditable Lou Christie imitation.

Speaking of Lou Christie, here he is with "Riding In My Van." This is my personal favorite on side two. Much attention has been paid to texture here, especially the unusual three-phase chorus which stacks its soaring vocal on top of sleigh bells, fuzz guitar, harpsichord, and some very solid, late-period Beatles-style drumming.

Roger McGuinn, of the original Byrds, makes his bid for a beach house in the stratosphere with "Draggin'," a hot rod song about racing Boeing 747s cross-country. Except for Bruce Johnston's vocal tracks, everything here seems improvised and a little confused. Charles Lloyd (Celebration) on sax does not help matters. I prefer "Ding Dang."

Bruce and Terry ride again in a previous incarnation, the Rip Chords, as "Hey Little Cobra" roars across the speakers. This record was modeled after "409" and "Shut Down," and it shows. I think the obvious

152

contrivance was debilitating to Bruce, who sounds positively bored on the refrain "shuddem dowwwnnn." A fun song nonetheless.

Bottoming out side two is a slightly amateurish offering called "Draggin' Wagon" by the Surfer Girls. That's right, an all-girl group. Can they play? Well, yeah, pretty good in fact. However, they cannot sing. The fact that they do not attempt to make harmony is probably in their favor. "Johnny B. Goode" is the song here, getting the "Surfin' U.S.A." treatment, sort-of. I don't like this one.

Side three opens with Walter Egan's "Hot Summer Nights." On the surface there doesn't seem to be a very obvious connection to the theme of this collection. This track is typical of the new California sound as made popular by the Eagles and Fleetwood Mac. What is not so obvious is that the production ideas and harmonic structures are no different from the old California sound.

Both old and new sounds merge on Ricci Martin's "Stop Look Around." A good song, a good singer, and a very good treatment by producers Carl Wilson and Billy Hinsche make this, and the rest of Martin's album *Beached* a worthwhile investment, particularly now that it can be found for $2.99 in the cut-out racks. On the negative side, there seems to have been some remixing done here, resulting in the lead vocal being boosted unnecessarily.

Jan and Dean's "Yellow Balloon" is actually just Dean, if I remember correctly. This version blows away the competition (a rival version beat it to the charts) with its vocals and personality. A charming recording.

My favorite cut on side three is "Swanee River" by Fresh. Actually a British group, this bunch could pass for the Tokens, not only for their vocal sound, but also in the case of this cut, for their arranging. The rhythm track has a very definitive Hawthorne feel to it. It's a nice companion to "Surfin' Down The Swanee River" by the Honeys and "South Bay Surfer" by the Beach Boys.

The Hondells' "Just One More Chance" reminds me of the Mamas and The Papas, whose records often displayed textural leanings toward

Phil Spector and Brian. The lead vocalist sounds a bit like Gary Puckett.

The big guns are brought out on side four, beginning with "Let Me Make Love To You" by Flo and Eddie, who in real life are Howard Kaylan and Mark Volman of the Turtles. This is a strong piece. Tension builds in the verses as two instrumental ideas vie for control, finally conceding to the chorus with all stops pulled out. While Flo and Eddie retain their own style, there are several nods to the master here.

Next we have one of Brian Wilson's last projects with American Spring (Marilyn Wilson and Diane Rovell), "Shyin' Away." This jaunty little song is well worth the price that some avid collectors have placed on it, as Brian's influence is pervasive. This is a great cut, worth the purchase of the entire set.

Jackie DeShannon's "Boat To Sail" is a pleasant ride down a calm river with low-key accompaniment and a lyrical reference to Brian and his music. The harmony vocals are credited to Brian and Marilyn Wilson, yet many would dispute that claim by pointing to the rough, sometimes embarrassing efforts made by Brian on his own behalf (more or less) during the same period of time. I prefer to argue that Brian Wilson would have been given free reign to improvise his own harmonies, and that his parts would not be the pedestrian block chords evident here.

"Don't Worry Baby" by Keller and Webb is given unusual treatment here with respect to the melody and modality of the original. The rewritten second verse, as utilized by B.J. Thomas and California Music, is used here, as is a full string section. There is a nice instrumental break built around a syncopated figured bass, which serves as a middle eight.

The Blue Rose's "My Impersonal Life," which closes the set, reminds me of Dennis Wilson circa *Carl and the Passions* or *Holland*. The spatial and textural qualities of its arrangement are a little heavy-handed, but still effective.

All in all, this is an important set, of more than passing interest to collectors and Beach Boy aficionados. My only complaint is that the liner notes are insufficiently informative with regard to recording dates, locations, producers, personnel, etc. Overlook any of my gripes, however, and buy this record.

album review:
law and order

By Gary Gidman

(Originally published in February 1982)

Lindsey Buckingham's recent solo effort *Law And Order* is a highly original work by a very individualistic artist. Arguably the brains behind Fleetwood Mac's last couple of LP projects, he is also an avid fan of Brian Wilson, and not afraid to say so (evidenced by the remake of "Farmer's Daughter" which his band released last year).

Law And Order seems less notable for the content of the songs (although there are some strong ones included) than for the arrangements. In a production sense, Buckingham seems to prefer a basic three- or four-position panning scheme, which clusters several tracks on top of one another in your ear, implying the density of Phil Spector's "Wall of Sound." However, the use of reverb or "plate" echo is almost always deferred here. Instead, tape echo or electronic delay is employed, creating a drier, subtly harsher, more "contemporary" sound. This is something of a nod to the "New Wave" school of music that is very popular in L.A. these days.

The arrangements, however, show the influence of Wilson. Each song on *Law And Order* is treated as a textural entity, rather than as a vehicle for a singer or guitar soloist. "Guitar hero" histrionics are confined to one track only. Buckingham creates a distinct textural setting for the mood of each song, using many of his trademark Big Mac guitar sounds, electronic piano and vibes, and various studio tricks (such as recording instruments at half speed so that when played back at normal speed the pitch is an octave higher and the timbre is unusual). The style is hard to define, but instantly recognizable, often yielding subtle similarities to his work with Fleetwood Mac.

Not so subtle, however, is Buckingham's employment of vocals, which are a stubborn, very stylized, and very respectful tip of his hat to Brian Wilson's arranging legacy. I say stubborn because vocals like this are not considered in the music business to be stylistically "contemporary," and therefore not conducive to mega-sales.

"Trouble," which garnered substantial airplay recently as a single, is only modestly representative in this sense. Two choral blocks of harmony ("Think I'm in trouble" and "Don't know what to do") barely overlap one another to make the song's refrain. A more telling example is "Bwana," which, after repeated listenings, brings to mind Brian's "Lana." Here we have one block of nonsense syllables in the verse ("Rah tatatah") and a wordless "Ahh" block, which almost passes for some kind of synthesized keyboard and embellishes the chorus. This is followed by a voice solo, possibly a kazoo, but I say a voice miked through a synthesizer or distortion unit or both, so that it barely resembles a human voice at all, except for inhalations between phrases.

Elsewhere we find "Shadow Of The West," featuring a solo voice disguised by echo, which follows the song's guitar motif around as if attached by a lariat. "Mary Lee Jones" seems rather Beatlesque instrumentally, but sports massed harmonies and a bass vocal in its chorus. There is a charmingly lugubrious cover of the old standard "September Song" and a straightforward remake of the country chestnut "Satisfied Mind." My personal favorite, "It Was I," a tune by songwriter Gary Paxton, is given a calliope-like bed of electric keyboards, and sounds as if it would be very much at home on side two of *The Beach Boys Love You*.

Its occasional quirkiness may seem a hindrance upon first listening, but time and attention will reveal *Law And Order* to be a work of undoubted originality which owes no small part of its appeal to the genius of Brian Wilson and happily acknowledges that debt. It is recommended.

surfer girl

By Don Cunningham

(Originally published in December 1978)

You are the super 1962 talent scout, and a couple of guys named Morgan and Wilson hand you a tape of a song called "Surfer Girl." A rather harmless little ditty—but worth a recording contract? Give Mr. Venet some credit. Would you have discerned in that performance what would eventually become America's most successful vocal group? Let's listen to it.

In the early recording (the Hite Morgan Candix track), somewhat loose harmonies and a too-slowed 4/4 rhythm simply cannot belie the song's melodic greatness. "Almost a capella" might describe the production, as the boys are accompanied by only a steady "skipping" triplet beat, which seems to emanate from the likes of a trashcan lid, and throbbing bass, which does little more than cue each chord. To round out this garage production, a faint electric guitar picks crude arpeggios, audible about a quarter of the time. Again, the harmonic mix of voices is uneven. Yet the careful listener will detect the promise of the Beach Boys harmonic sound that would be polished over the next two years.

Brian's later production for Capitol was the proof, and, in 1963, propelled "Surfer Girl" to #7 on the singles chart (backed by a Candix compatriot, "Little Deuce Coupe"). This version cured any and all ills of the earlier "Surfer Girl." However, all changes were really very slight, indicating two things: that the original was close to superlative and that Brian realized this and did not lose any of the original's virtues via radical alteration. Nonetheless, there was one large add-on. From the beautiful falsetto fadeout, Brian fashioned an intro that he would later dub "the most beautiful introduction to any song." It soars with sentiment and gives the song a cyclic quality, which enhances the idea of an eternal kind of love, as revealed in the lyrics.

Brian moves up slightly from what sounds like a D-flat major tonic in the original to a happier D-major. A slight increase in the tempo and tighter harmonies finally dispose of a somewhat maudlin aspect, while maintaining a sentiment filled with child-like hope and pious intention. The harmonies attain fruition. In the original lead, "We could ride the surf..." is accompanied by a ringing soprano "Ahh..." The key word is "accompanied." The cleaner harmony in the final version seems to surround the lyric, not accompany it—fusing the subconscious refrain to the vocalized thought.

The instrumental production remains modest while much improved. Steady triplets are offered by bass, light guitar, and cymbal, producing a sense of urgency while covering a wide emotional spectrum. To finish the story, graceful bass leaps during chord changes in the A sections provide a security that is offset by guitar-plucking in the B sections. The sound is now professional.

No grand ideas are at work in the basic structure of "Surfer Girl." It is AABA with a bridged modulation to E-flat in the final A section. In the B section, syncopation of the final syllable of "together" and a melisma on "grow" provide clues to the possibility of adolescent angst.

There is a quality in this song that gives it the feel of a classic more so than a song such as "Girls on the Beach." "Help Me, Rhonda" is undisputedly a classic, yet not in quite the same way that "Surfer Girl" is. After all, if you play your entire Beach Boys collection for your mother, chances are she'll choose "Surfer Girl" as her favorite. The reasons are many. The melodic line enhances the lyrics powerfully. Up-and-down A sections portray the naïve hopes (up on "do you") and shaky confidence (down on "love me") of infatuation. The lyrics can even stand on their own. "Little surfer, little one" evokes not only an angelic surfer girl, but also a likable boy in thrall.

> **If you play your entire Beach Boys collection for your mother, chances are she'll choose "Surfer Girl" as her favorite.**

Sing the first few lines. The beauty and evocativeness are rooted in simplicity. Note how the matched descending intervals and lack of chromatics combine to give the steep opening line a singsong charac-

> **It soars with sentiment and gives the song a cyclic quality, which enhances the idea of an eternal kind of love.**

ter which a child can repeat. A kind of infantilism is at work here. Very potent as a songwriting tool, this tone is only successful insofar as it carefully taps a deep, collective human experience. And there can not be too much humor present, or it slides into parody. Buddy Holly was very successful with his stylized use of this idea. His "baby" vocal technique and his lyrics would frequently generate that child-like (but not childish) feeling: "Pretty pretty pretty pretty Peggy Sue."

In "Surfer Girl," all the musical elements fit together perfectly, producing a song that, after the first few notes, breathes with musical necessity. One could go on and on about its virtues. Feel free to do that while keeping one final thought in mind: this is possibly the very first Beach Boy song Brian Wilson wrote.

car crazy cutie

By Don Cunningham

(Originally published in June 1980)

There was a period in 1963 when Brian Wilson—kid just out of high school, modest practical joker, AM radio nut, sensitive artist—could excitedly summon all the resources of his memory—the nights, the places, the feelings, the songs—dash into a recording studio, and, using L.A.'s best studio musicians, create a song that was accessible to 10 million kids across the country.

"Car Crazy Cutie" is such a song. It was crafted for the *Little Deuce Coupe* album of 1963, an album filled with such songs and unjustly ignored over the years because of its overt automobile themes. I would like to argue the case for this simple type of song, which relies more on an overall sense of fun than on particular vocal, instrumental, or production statements. It is the kind of song Brian had trouble coming up with, or chose not to create, for many years (late '60s-early '70s). Fans who yearn for the old sound (fans such as new wave artists) yearn for songs such as "Car Crazy Cutie." This is the sound to which Wilson possibly has referred when stating "I like the old songs best."

There are many reasons for liking a song, but what one has to appreciate in "Car Crazy Cutie" is a sense of the hand of Providence in the result. It would seem that the fates handed Brian a finished product even as he labored a good artist's labor. After all, here was a young man with no formal training in production and little in composition, brazenly aping Dion's "Runaround Sue" in structure and style and ending up with a Beach Boys song—somehow removed totally from Dion's conception in time and space.

There are revealing differences between "Car Crazy Cutie" and "Runaround Sue"—especially in the production, engineering, and manufacturing advances that made any '60s or '70s remake of a '50s hit sound "fuller."

For example, unlike "Runaround Sue," in "Car Crazy Cutie" you can actually hear the bass, and the harmony actually sounds like live voices. The technological advances that make for such changes/improvements have been minimized by those who have analyzed the progress of popular music in general over the past 30 years. Consider the idea of hearing Sinatra's "It Was A Very Good Year" coming from a 78-rpm record.

In the opening bars of "Car Crazy Cutie," Wilson constructs a B-major progression with Beach Boy voices (B-B7-E-F-sharp). Today we can say this is revealing; back then it just sounded good. Of special note is Dennis' voice, which, used prominently, gives the vocal collage a flat sound, good for a car song, good for a Dion song. Brian has the lead, however, and as the song proceeds, gives it his own Dion-best, tying notes together with vocal slurring in the Dion-Darin tradition of rock and roll singing.

> Of special note is Dennis' voice, which, used prominently, gives the vocal collage a flat sound, good for a car song.

What else is going on? Not much, except for a powerful ascending rock bass and simple but perfect drumming. Some mixed-down surf guitar follows the beat throughout. The Ramones wouldn't have any trouble with this arrangement. In fact, the Ramones likely consider "Car Crazy Cutie" and other primordial Beach Boys songs to be great stuff. Many people are surprised to learn of an allegiance of new wave and punk musicians to Brian and the Beach Boys. But this is why. Brian understood the beauty of the basics as opposed to the gloss of the baroque. In "Car Crazy Cutie," he went little farther than did Dion in "Runaround Sue." Wilson used better engineering and Beach Boy voices, but knew that beauty lay in that simple B-B7 progression and rock beat. Simple. Because of that sensibility, Brian will always be linked to the earlier defining rock and roll era.

In a more obvious but less fundamental way Wilson is linked to the '50s era by his use of nonsense syllables—in this case "doo run run." Note how such nonsense syllables, in a certain school of songwriting, are as acceptable as any "real" word in Webster's. This is a suitable lead into a second song I would like to discuss—"Pamela Jean," by the Survivors (released in 1964; Capitol 5102)—which is essentially "Car Crazy Cutie" with different lyrics. The first

> **Many people are surprised to learn of an allegiance of new wave and punk musicians to Brian and the Beach Boys.**

thing a listener notices about "Pamela Jean" is that Brian uses different nonsense syllables at the start ("wat, wa da doo..."). "Pamela Jean" then proceeds with an overall sound that is rougher, or busier, that that of "Car Crazy Cutie."

The structures and key systems of the two tracks are identical. Also similar are the finger snaps, bass lines, ending falsetto (mixed down in "Pamela Jean"), and a capella vocal intro (which returns for the songs' endings). As for differences, "Pamela Jean" sports a horn component that displaces the "bare" bass of "Car Crazy Cutie." That, along with a richer mix of instruments, hand claps, and less-resolved vocal harmonies, contributes to the rougher sound texture I mentioned.

Both songs suffer from uninspired lyrics. That might account for the failure of both to rise to a place of prominence in the Beach Boys catalog. Yet both songs are top-notch rock and roll. If "Pamela Jean" is memorable for its horns and rock bass, and "Car Crazy Cutie" is memorable for its strong harmonies and rock bass, a third version of this song ought to be remembered for its humorous lyrics. I am referring to "Muscle Beach Party," which was recorded by both Annette Funicello and Frankie Avalon. This nearly identical song features the structure and harmonics of the other two, produced, I gather, under the umbrella of the company that created the film *Muscle Beach Party*.

Roger Christian penned the lyrics for "Car Crazy Cutie," Brian likely wrote the words for "Pamela Jean," and Gary Usher got into the act by supplying lyrics for "Muscle Beach Party." The music is by Brian Wilson.

To sum up: by utilizing better production techniques, technical advances, and Beach Boy harmonies (with their sociological attributes) in a song that is essentially orthodox rock and roll, Brian Wilson strengthened the rock and roll fortress in a modest way with lasting results.

it's a beautiful day

By Don Cunningham

(Originally published in September 1979)

Ever notice that Beach Boy songs that do not involve Brian Wilson often sound impressive at first, yet over a period of a few months diminish in promise like a wife of Henry VIII — eventually making their way to the song basket labeled "mediocre?" It seems that "It's A Beautiful Day," from the soundtrack of the motion picture *Americathon*, may be such a song. Yet I wonder…does closer inspection of this track reveal some musical steps that might quietly point to good news? Might the old trend be overcome?

The total synthesis of elements in the sections of "It's A Beautiful Day" in which Carl sings are impressive and significant. His hot vocal and the accompanying harmonies display a renewed understanding of how melody, harmony, and rhythm are very much dependent on each other (or should be). The result in this chorus is a heady sound that the Beach Boys minus Brian Wilson have not produced in the past.

Al's and Mike's vocal parts in the verses put me to sleep. Al's strong style and a jumping rhythm behind Mike's lines don't make up for the uninspired writing and arranging. Still, even if "It's A Beautiful Day" is released as a single only to die a quick death, there will remain virtue in some of the music—and therefore hope. This, along with signs that Brian Wilson will continue to improve (at one point last summer, a "Brian" side of the next album was proposed), should keep us going.

goin' on

By Don Cunningham

(Originally published in March 1980)

Hey, what's goin' on? That's not Brian on four-track. Sounds like Bruce Johnston on 24-track. Those harmonies on the new single are dense. Maybe too dense. This is more overdubbing than we have come to expect from Brian Wilson. Yet sources have conspired to make me believe that it is Brian's work.

The production is unlike the man who revels in certain sounds: tambourines, sleigh bells, synthesizer — the Spector homage, the sense of rock and roll history. "Goin' On" does not have those qualities, yet it is very strong.

I believe the strength lies chiefly in the songwriting. Melody and rhythm collaborate on a plot that moves the listener up and down, back and forth, with a spirit of soulful fun. Carl's voice, the lyricism, the family harmony, Brian's "goin' ah-on," and a refreshing song structure are all enjoyable for the Brian watchers. Yet, for the public in an age of sparse new wave statements, this texture may be too much.

I get a sense of taking stock in this production — as if the group has seriously weighed its strengths and weaknesses, has surveyed the commercial scene, and is searching for a synthesis of strengths and expectations. Brian's melodic gift still is rarely equaled. On the other hand, his voice has changed, and his finger can't find the record-buyers' pulse. The Beach Boys have farther to go, but they have taken a step in the right direction.

good or bad, glad or sad

By Tom Ekwurtzel

(Originally published in March 1980)

When you come right down to it, among other things, the Beach Boys are cult figures. Unlike some bigger cults, however, there do not seem to be enough Beach Boy loyalists to move a new Beach Boys album into the top ten, or even to hold one of those fan conventions like they have for the Beatles or "Star Trek."

At recent conventions celebrating those just-mentioned phenomena, I noticed that votes were taken in "worst of" categories. For instance, at the "Star Trek" meeting, the episode voted as worst was "The Garden of Eden," where a group of hippie types invaded the Enterprise and called Kirk "Herbert." At the Beatles exposition, the worst Beatles song turned out to be "Mr. Moonlight" from *Beatles '65*.

The point, evidently, is to poke fun at our heroes. Things shouldn't be so serious that we dare not laugh. These people are supposed to entertain. Therefore this article is more a labor of love than anything else. With that I present my personal top five choices for worst Beach Boys track of all time.

1) "Love Surrounds Me" (from *L.A. (Light Album)*): An absolute chore to listen to. The arrangement is dense, senseless, plodding, and boring. Repetition is usually a potent aspect of the Beach Boys. Here it is dull, lifeless and meandering nowhere.

2) "Hold On Dear Brother" (from *Carl and The Passions: So Tough*): Come on. This wasn't even the Beach Boys. A shameful grade for that sacrilege alone. Ricky Fataar and Blondie Chaplin tried to be Brian with all sorts of chords, but unlike him, they gave us no brilliant melody and no interesting idiosyncrasies.

3) "Let's Put Our Hearts Together" (from *The Beach Boys Love You*): Brian tries a duet with his wife Marilyn, and hers is a voice which need not be on plastic. Brian here is a commercial for the anti-smoking league. No redeeming value in sight.

4) "In The Still Of The Night" (from *15 Big Ones*): The worst vocal performance on any Beach Boy record. At times, I find Dennis' flat growl soulful, but here it is just embarrassing.

5) "Bull Session With The Big Daddy" (from *Today*): This spoken-word track makes the list mostly because *Today* is otherwise a stunning album. This is like stepping from James Joyce into Fanny Farmer.

In reviewing the old albums, I think it's important to realize that many of the flaws and fillers were justified. They were errors of naivete, reflecting in a very sincere way the lack of pretension which is a cornerstone of the Beach Boys. The songs sounded as if they were a blast to record ("Drive-In" and "South Bay Surfer" come to mind), and listeners could sense that. Sincerity was so real then. Nothing can again capture the charm of someone coughing in the middle of "Wendy" (during the break), or of Dennis stumbling during his Christmas message ("And if you hap-happen to be listening...").

> I start to realize that time may be doing the Beach Boys in just as it's doing us all in.

I suppose I pale listening to some recent Beach Boys material. I can barely listen to Carl's vocal on "Sweet Sunday Kind Of Love." This guy can crank it up and instead they opt for schmaltz. "Everyone's In Love With You" is worse. My spirits were flowing just fine on side one of *Holland* and side two of *Surf's Up* until I ran into "The Beaks Of Eagles" and "A Day In The Life Of A Tree." Why so serious? Where's the fun?

This article began as a good-humored jab at my favorite band, and now I start to realize that time may be doing the Beach Boys in just as it's doing us all in. Is that the way these things must go? We're the first

generation to watch rock stars grow old. Elvis got to be a drag while Buddy Holly remains glorious. Mick Jagger is appearing to age, but Jimi Hendrix is an image to behold.

The Beach Boys? I want to give 'em up for dead. Forget about it; California falls into the sea. But I'll sit through 1,000 plays of "Goin' South" for one listen to "Good Timin'" or "She's Got Rhythm." And what if Brian teamed up with Tony Asher again? Or Van Dyke Parks? Nah. I'm not so sure it actually happened the first time around.

hanging 10

By Don Cunningham

(Originally published in September 1981)

Both Bo Derek and the Beach Boys got a lot of exposure in the summer of 1981. Yet, after all the interviews, media-shaping, and controversy, a naked Mrs. Derek seen on the screen and a medley of chopped-up Beach Boy songs heard on the radio end up as vicarious experiences. Bo Derek did not deliver a new hairstyle this summer, and the Beach Boys failed to introduce a new song.

To make matters worse, Brian Wilson seemed to approach another low point. His appearance included a bloated stomach, neglected long hair, and, during a Hartford performance, hands that shook like leaves on a tree. His singing on stage did not improve, and his impatience increased, leading to a flare-up at L.A.'s Greek Theatre on July 17.

Carl Wilson quit the group this summer. Dennis and Mike were at odds yet again. The band recorded no new material. They became an oldies act in concert.

What is there to be optimistic about? A lesson from the past: the Beach Boys can rally. Out of an environment of failed singles at the very end of the Sixties came the album *Sunflower*. From the desperate scene of half-filled concert halls in the early Seventies emerged the momentous tours of 1974-1975. After Brian Wilson's production neglect in the first half of the Seventies came the commercially successful *15 Big Ones* and artistically impressive *The Beach Boys Love You*.

Something in the blood relationship and the Wilson personality keeps the Beach Boys going. They are an organic group. A principle of science states that a system will readjust itself to reduce pressure. In the case of the organism called the Beach Boys, the resources needed to make the adjustment exist. Listen to the music.

175

meet me tonight
in atlantic city

By Geoffrey Himes

(Originally published in February 1983)

M*usician Player & Listener* magazine had assigned me to write a long profile of Carl Wilson, with an emphasis on the musical evolution of the Beach Boys.

So I drove from Baltimore to Atlantic City. It was my first visit to the crumbling resort town now gilded with casinos. I fought my way through the lines of tourist buses and arrived at Resorts International Casino & Hotel. Inside was an unreal world of blue-haired ladies in plastic straw hats, bright orange carpeting, garish chandeliers, and buzzing uniformed employees. In the center was the casino—a gymnasium-sized room crammed with lines of slot machines constantly fed by bug-eyed vacationers. It was any video game parlor expanded to nightmarish proportions.

Penny Staples from Rogers & Cowan, the Beach Boys' publicity firm, found me in the lobby and took me to lunch. After a while, Bruce Johnston and some friends joined us.

Bruce indicated that the much-rumored album *Cousins, Friends & Brothers* is nowhere near completion. He implied that Brian was in very bad shape right now and not ready to work on a major project. He said that a live version of Del Shannon's "Runaway," recorded in Cleveland, had been considered as a single. But when Al Jardine—whose project it was—heard the mix, he realized it wasn't up to par. "It didn't have enough of our signature," Bruce explained.

As I pressed him about Brian's current state, he replied, "Guys like you are real sad that we've turned into a big money-making machine,

177

that Brian is not making new music like the old music. But Brian's legacy is still there, and millions of people still respond to it. And we carry on that legacy. Is there anything wrong with that? I mean, everyone's sad about Brian. It's like Stravinsky retiring at 28. Brian was like Rachmaninoff; he was a great pianist as well as a great composer. Brian didn't need the recording industry. He still would have been heard if he had worked with symphony orchestras. His music still would have come out. You and I are glad that he did have records, but he didn't need them. I'm not sure I want to make another record unless it's going to be an important record. Either Brian will have to write some material up to his own standards, or we'll have to find some other material up to the same standards. The tunes have to be there. Otherwise, why bother? I've got better things to do with two months of my life. There's no thrill for me anymore in being in the studio on a Sunday night at two in the morning. I'd rather be at home, talking to my wife, playing with my kids, and going to bed at 11."

> "Brian's legacy is still there, and millions of people still respond to it. And we carry on that legacy. Is there anything wrong with that?" – Bruce Johnston

"It's exciting when you're young and coming up, but after you've done it, you get older and other things become important. Unless, of course, it's an important record. The same thing is true of the solo records. How many stiffs can you make before you get the message? Making a stiff is a humbling experience; it's happened to all of us. Dennis got his ass kicked; I got my ass kicked; Mike got his ass kicked; Carl got his ass kicked."

At 3:30, I went up to Carl's room, and we talked for two and a half hours. This was the fifth time I'd interviewed Carl, so he has gotten to know me and was quite forthcoming in the interview.

I asked him how his demands had been met so that he rejoined the tour, after having spent much of 1981 and early 1982 on a self-imposed exile from the band. He said he had to compromise to meet the guys halfway. He had insisted that the bass player be fired and that Ed Carter be rehired in his place. That was done. He also insisted on a

week's worth of rehearsals before the band left for the tour. He got a lot of resistance on this, but once everyone showed up, they really got into it, he said.

He agreed to play the resorts that had already been booked on this tour, but not on any future tours. Bruce had sworn in the lunchroom that he hated playing resorts so much he would never do them again. Carl noted that all the guys hated them, and he would strongly push that they stop doing them next year.

Carl also got some different songs such as "I Can Hear Music," "Darlin'," and "Disney Girls" into the band's concert repertoire. He also led the way on John Fogerty's "Rockin' All Over The World," which will be featured on his forthcoming solo album.

In addition to seven Carl Wilson-Myrna Smith-Schilling compositions, the solo album will also include the Fogerty song, the Coasters' "Young Blood," Billy Hinsche's "One More Night Alone," and John Hall's "What You Do To Me." The album is finished, but Carl and his manager, Jerry Schilling, decided to wait until January so that the

179

album won't get lost in the pre-Christmas releases. Timothy B. Schmidt, Burton Cummings, Billy Hinsche, and Jeff Baxter all appear on the album.

The Beach Boys' show was at 7:30. Dennis had been traveling with the band, but was back in California to be with his girlfriend, who recently had a baby. Carl, Brian, Mike, Al and Bruce were joined on stage by drummer Mike Kowalski, guitarists Jeff Foskett and Adrian Baker, bassist Ed Carter, and keyboardist Mike Meros. After a ragged version of "It's OK," the band segued into a gorgeous version of "I Can Hear Music." Carl sounded better than I have ever heard him, especially his R&B belting on "Darlin'" and his smooth crooning on "God Only Knows." Carl and Foskett added strong guitar breaks. Whatever you may feel about Mike Love's political role in the band's internal struggles, he's still a great singer.

Brian sat at the piano for every song, but played only intermittently and sang even less. Most of the time he would sit there with his hands dangling at his sides. He would occasionally mouth the lyrics without singing them, and would glance at the band and then the crowd as if searching for something. He seemed a bemused spectator at the interaction between band and crowd over his own songs.

Geoffrey Himes has written about music for the Washington Post, National Public Radio, Rolling Stone, Musician, Request, Downbeat, Country Music Magazine, No Depression and many other publications. He has contributed to The Encyclopedia of Country Music and the Rolling Stone Jazz & Blues Album Guide.

let's go away for awhile and pet sounds

By Don Cunningham

(Originally published in December 1980)

"Let's Go Away For Awhile" is the better of these two instrumental tracks from the 1966 *Pet Sounds* album. Better because it more successfully blends into the album, extending while exacting the thematic consciousness—the rigors of young love and early self-image. This is an all-important criterion for criticism of a *Pet Sounds* track, since the work is commonly touted as the first great concept album.

Who should go away for awhile? The boy and girl. On the other hand, one asks, to whom do the "pet sounds" belong? The answer is either to Brian Wilson or to the Beach Boys, not to the archetypal lovers. This is not as it should be. Although *Pet Sounds* is ultimately about Brian Wilson's persona, that fact should be found in higher levels of interpretation, not a song's face value.

Yet while "Let's Go Away For Awhile" contributes to the album's synthesis, "Pet Sounds" has its own virtues, marvelous qualities that seem to exist outside and despite the themes of the album with the same title. "Pet Sounds" (the song) offers a glimpse into the world of Brian Wilson via the sound textures that are indelibly Brian's. *Pet Sounds* (the album) is a journey through the world of Brian Wilson via a totally realized concept of theme, plot, and substance, expressed in music and lyrics.

Here is Wilson in an early 1967 interview:

> "I think that on *Pet Sounds* the track, "Let's Go Away For Awhile" is the most satisfying piece of music I've ever made. I applied a certain set of dynamics through the arrangement and the mixing and got a full musical extension of what I'd planned during the

earliest stages of the theme. I think the chord changes are very special. I've used a lot of musicians on the track, 12 violins (I guess fiddles is the hip phrase), piano, 4 saxes, oboe, vibes, and guitar with a Coke bottle on the strings for a semi-steel guitar effect. Also I used two basses and percussion.

The total effect is...let's go away for awhile, which is something everyone in the world must have said at some time or other. Nice thought. Most of us don't go away, but it's still a nice thought. The track was supposed to be on the backing for a vocal, but I decided to leave it alone."

Brian has never been as tonally or rhythmically adventurous as in "Let's Go Away For Awhile." Not that it brings to mind the aleatory of John Cage. Rather, it maintains a popular music feel even as it ignores the pathways of ordinary popular songs. For this Wilson can be included in a small group of peers, from George Gershwin to Stevie Wonder, who successfully redefined popular music by integrating fundamentally new ideas into songwriting, producing, and other creative aspects.

With regard to development of key, the songs of *Pet Sounds* can be arranged in two categories. The first group includes unsurprising key development, with basic chords spelling usual Western cadences. Here I would place "I'm Waiting For The Day," "I Know There's An Answer," "Wouldn't It Be Nice?" "You Still Believe In Me," and perhaps "God Only Knows" and "Here Today." The second group includes songs that aspire more noticeably to leave notions of Western cadences behind. These employ all sorts of major chords, sixths, sevenths, ninths, and elevenths, and stay away from common progressions such as I-IV-V-I. "That's Not Me," "Caroline No," "Don't Talk," "I Just Wasn't Made For These Times," "Pet Sounds," and "Let's Go Away For Awhile" are such songs.

> **Brian has never been as tonally or rhythmically adventurous as in "Let's Go Away For Awhile."**

"Let's Go Away For Awhile" opens with bass, vibes, and guitar establishing not a simple F, but a broader, more complex ninth of the chord. After six bars of half notes and whole notes, with these instruments delicately moving through D, E-flat, A-flat9, and B-flat-major7, the piano and guitar play five bars of sensitive eighth notes—where the chords become stranger yet somehow better. This A section is repeated with added violins extending the theme—a kind of complex ordinariness from which one might wish to "go away."

Then an abrupt horn bridge plays a trick by faking a cadence that would resolve musically the first section. It jumps from C to C-sharp, ushering in the next part of the song, which is in the brand new key of D. The time signature also changes here, and a slowed-down "music box" theme is played by vibes and guitar, accentuated by percussion. This second part has its own developmental section wherein violins vacillate emotionally between an almost traditional G-major7 and A11. Drum voices become more prominent as the end approaches, and, as this last section fades, those drums become a jarring rhythmic foil to the violins, which are indeed "going away for awhile."

The bass is, more than any other instrument or voice, including drums, the beat element in "Let's Go Away For Awhile." It is nearly a percussion instrument. On the other hand, those drums heard mostly at the end, and other sounds usually regarded as percussion, are more properly called textural elements in the song. Not that this idea is new. Throughout the album *Pet Sounds*, the following goal is attained more completely than anywhere else: instruments and voices lose their individual identities as distinct

> Instruments and voices lose their individual identities as distinct pieces of the band, thus better offering their sounds to aesthetic and artistic interpretations.

pieces of the band, thus better offering their sounds to aesthetic and artistic interpretations. A drum becomes an emotion. A voice becomes a person.

Without a doubt, what continues in the song "Pet Sounds," despite its faults regarding theme, is a bold advance in songwriting and production—as in "Let's Go Away For Awhile." These instrumentals are light-years away from 1963's "Stoked" and 1964's "After The Game." "Pet Sounds" first attacks the listener with percussion and an intriguing and powerful bass theme. The theme is a standard cadence from F to B-flat, establishing the key. It becomes stronger as horns support it.

There is a sense of contrapuntal drama between the low bass and the melody, played on guitar. In the verse, the bass seems to win out, for, as the guitar rises then comes back down, it is underscored by the bass descent which draws the listener back to the F/B-flat hook.

Background guitars spice up the harmonic sequences, setting disparate chords against the progression and producing a sort of agitation. Along with the weird percussion and rich guitar melody, these chords create an interesting texture, to say the least.

As in "Let's Go Away For Awhile," the percussion in "Pet Sounds" acts like an exclamation point at the end of phrases, and, in the end, rises to the fore. After twice through the basic run of "Pet Sounds," the percussion is given full reign in a strange interlude that seems to include bongos and chopped horn blasts. It feels like a reduction to raw instincts—which yield to a different kind of ending and fade. The jazzy ending is unlike Wilson. Dueling guitars fade out with the theme in a counterpoint of strong musical urgency. This has less of a primal feel; it "sounds" more refined than the previous percussion part, yet still comes across as basic instinct.

The song "Pet Sounds" can evoke Brian Wilson's personality more directly than can the rest of the album, since it is a departure from the developing theme. Rather than adding to the story that the other songs support, "Pet Sounds" takes leave and, in a playful manner, gives us a collage of Wilson artistic urges—musical ideas that support themes in the other songs, and that are here presented in an objective environment.

Brian was well past Phil Spector when he composed these two songs—these textural statements—for *Pet Sounds*. He was on his own, going with his instincts, producing not a wall of sound, but a mature musical expressionism that was and is high art. Praise for *Pet Sounds* (the album) should not be simply for its early conceptual nature. The praise should go farther to acknowledge a total artistic synthesis, from songwriting to arranging, from playing, singing, and production to engineering. Brian did it without Mann and Weil writing the songs, without George Martin producing, and, to a large extent (certainly on these two songs), without the Beach Boys.

185

no better zephyr:
the beach boys live, march 20, 1980
By Neal Delaporta

(Originally published in March 1980)

The first summer breezes blew prematurely into Hartford, Connecticut on March 20. This meteorological magic was a result of the Beach Boys' visit to the insurance city. Almost 14,000 cheering fans of all ages greeted the group, and as the first powerful strains of "California Girls" pulsed through the air of the newly-refurbished Hartford Civic Center, those cheers escalated into shouts.

When the lights came up we found that Dennis was absent but Bruce was a Beach Boy again. Brian lent his incomparable presence to the entire set. Besides the five Beach Boys, the musical ensemble was comprised of Jim Guercio on bass, Bobby Figueroa on drums and Mike Meros on keyboards. This musical amalgam was more than apt in their interpretation of the many classic Wilson tunes.

As for the repertoire, missing this night were "Peggy Sue," "Roller Skating Child," "It's OK," "Angel Come Home," and "You Are So Beautiful." Additions were simply "I Write The Songs," which Bruce did solo (as he did in New York last March), and a surprising "Long Tall Texan," which Mike introduced as "a song we have not done in fifteen years."

From a strictly theatrical standpoint, the show was impressive in many ways. First, the stage setting, amplification system, and concert grand piano were a strikingly stark, but hardly austere, regal, snow white. Adding to this brilliant effect was a well designed and well executed lighting display, which featured a cycloramic palm tree projection on the upstage screen during "Catch A Wave," and mood lighting for each of the evening's definitive musical "movements."

The band in general, and Mike Love in particular, seemed to establish a good rapport with their audience of (in Mike's words) "insurance types." Perhaps this was helped by the fact that this was the first rock concert held in the Civic Center since the repair of its collapsed roof, which Mike jokingly acknowledged ("Now if any song could bring the roof down, this next one...oops!").

Mike's pre-song antics were well-prepared, well-delivered, and well-received. For Al's "Lady Lynda," he gave his "classical music lesson" intro. For Bruce's "I Write The Songs," he gave his "music industry lesson" intro. He gave Carl's "God Only Knows" his *Pet Sounds*/sand-box intro. Finally, he chastised Glen Campbell for "blowing his chance for fame as a Beach Boy."

As a further sign of the performer-audience intimacy that had developed, Brian leaned into his microphone after "Long Tall Texan" and rasped "Now listen, who's better, Mick Jagger or Mike Love?" Whereupon Mike countered with "Who's better at songwriting, Paul McCartney or Brian Wilson?" The audience shouted what you might expect as Brian shouted "McCartney!"

Insofar as musical highlights are concerned, perhaps the only element that eclipsed the always-emotional encore of "Good Vibrations," "Barbara Ann" and "Fun, Fun, Fun" was the moving, magnificently rendered a capella coda of "Lady Lynda." Whether or not the reprise of this a capella portion was rehearsed, this was indeed the strongest and most effective the harmony has sounded in recent memory.

If it would have been possible for the "bigger and better" Hartford Civic Center to have a more special and sincere premier rock performance, this writer would be hard-pressed to imagine it. No better zephyr could have passed through town than the one that carried with it the Beach Boys.

album review:
rock 'n' roll city

By Don Cunningham

(Originally published in February 1983)

This newly recorded album of twelve songs has a lot to offer to fans of the Beach Boys. In addition to one new Beach Boys track (a cover of The Mamas and The Papas' "California Dreamin'"), it features six tracks on which Mike Love sings or shares the lead vocal, and one song featuring Bruce Johnston on lead. Also contributing are past or present Beach Boys associates Dean Torrence, Daryl Dragon, Terry Melcher, Adrian Baker, and Jeff Foskett.

The twelve tunes contained here – all remakes of '60s and '50s classics – provide an array of musical ideas. With the possible exception of "Sugar Shack," this is a program of exceptionally popular oldies with musical themes that are well balanced and interesting. Throughout this energetic LP, weaker aspects of singing, playing, and arranging are redeemed by refreshing displays of singing styles, vocal and instrumental motifs, and production values. Vocal harmony is the name of the game for most of *Rock 'n' Roll City*; backgrounds are full and tight, and some contrapuntal vocal movements are served up.

Daryl Dragon, the erstwhile "Captain of the Keyboards" from the Beach Boys touring band of the early '70s, is credited with producing eight of the tracks on *Rock 'n' Roll City*. His synthesizer and general keyboard arrangements have an up-to-date feeling, and he sometimes attempts to be rather creative. On the whole, however, his productions are simple and crisp, with a very pop feel, and they always allow the vocals to dominate the tracks.

189

The stronger cuts belong to the new duo of Mike (Love) and Dean (Torrence), who deliver an exciting, modernized rendition of Lou Christie's "Lightning Strikes," and a well vocalized, male version of the Angels' "My Boyfriend's Back" (here rechristened "Her Boyfriend's Back").

Mike's solo "Da Doo Ron Ron" features the unfortunate disco handclaps that we've come to expect from its producer, Adrian Baker. Despite the uninspired rhythm track, the recording comes alive with vocal counterpoint. One can picture Baker in his home studio in England, painstakingly overdubbing each voice. But compared to the sumptu- ousness of the Spector original, Baker's version of "Da Doo Ron Ron" rings hollow.

On Mike's version of "The Locomotion," the rhythm track is again uninspired, yet a kind of white soul answer harmony is a saving grace, even causing Mike's nasal lead vocal to take on a slightly soulful charac- ter of its own.

The Beach Boys' "California Dreaming (sic)," although obviously not a Brian Wilson production, contains some nifty production ideas. Pro- duced by Bruce Johnston, Terry Melcher and Al Jardine, it opens with a beautiful, full, "folk rock" acoustic guitar, and metamorphoses into a somewhat new wave/disco feel, as far as the rhythm track goes. The Beach Boys' vocals are fine, although I hear Bruce Johnston in the background harmonies, and not Brian Wilson. The lead vocals stand out – an inspired

> After fooling with many formulas, it just may be that Mike Love has found the right road to take.

collaboration of Mike, Carl and Al. Since this is supposed to be a Beach Boys song, it should be criticized, despite its overall success, for its lack of Brian Wilson vocal arrangements, and a Brian Wilson rhythm track.

Johnston and Melcher also step forward under one of their old '60s monikers, The Rip Chords, for a version of Bryan Hyland's "Sealed With A Kiss," sung by Bruce.

Dean Torrence handles two of the four tracks not featuring any Beach Boys involvement. He puts much effort into his remake of "Baby Talk," with fuller sounding vocals and a pure imitation of Jan. "Wild Thing" is

only an average track, although, to be fair, there isn't much you can do with that song. Still, Dean's fans will revel in his tongue-in-cheek humor on this track, as well as the humor he adds to the lead vocal on Mike and Dean's "Her Boyfriend's Back."

To round out the album, the reformed Association puts inspired harmony into a version of the Left Banke's "Walk Away Renee," while Paul Revere & The Raiders provide a more than faithful remake of "96 Tears," with its beautiful and famous organ figures intact.

In the final analysis, *Rock 'n' Roll City* manages to present an enjoyable and coherent whole from an amalgam of unrelated songs and talents. One finds that the songs grow on you, revealing new aspects on repeat playings. Even more important is that this album delivers that classic feeling of rock and roll fun.

After fooling with many formulas, it just may be that Mike Love has found the right road to take, at least as far as a solo career is concerned. He needs to choose his lead vocals more carefully, though – a number of leads on *Rock 'n' Roll City* (especially "The Locomotion" and "The

Letter") lean toward a nasal-saccharine quality. He does better with "Lightning Strikes," "California Dreaming" and "Her Boyfriend's Back." He would be wise to ask for Brian Wilson's recommendations, since Brian's estimation of Mike's abilities is probably more accurate than Mike's own.

(*Editor's Note*: *Rock 'n' Roll City* was released on cassette by Radio Shack in 1983. An 11-track vinyl album, minus the Beach Boys track, surfaced shortly thereafter under the title *Mike & Dean Rock 'n' Roll Again*. The Beach Boys recording of "California Dreaming" featured on the *Rock 'n' Roll City* cassette is an earlier, different recording from the one that became a minor hit single in 1986 and was included on that year's *Made In U.S.A.* album.)

the little girl i once knew

By Don Cunningham

(Originally published in September 1981)

Brian Wilson was asked whether there was a song he had done that never got its due, and he replied as follows:

> "'The Little Girl I Once Knew'—I thought was done real beautifully, and it had a real fabulous introduction. I would do the lead voices again. I would do them a lot better. I would leave the introduction alone. I thought that was beautiful."

Brian's modesty is complete. He can discuss one of his works as if it were someone else's, say Phil Spector's. Brian will revel in the qualities of "The Little Girl I Once Knew" with the same boyish excitement and awe that you or I might express. He will not spell out those inspired devices he fashioned into the song, making it work, but he will say that the introduction is beautiful, leaving us with a simple understatement.

I remember when my older sister bought the single in 1965 (with picture sleeve). What sort of subliminal aural education was forcing itself upon me, at age 11, as I heard those strange chords, that jazzy bass line, those organ triplets? How was my sense of time and space increasing while counting to eight during the famous musical dead spot before the chorus?

There was tension. Things happened in "The Little Girl I Once Knew" that were problematic to the young mind. It was awfully different from "Do You Wanna Dance?" "The Little Girl I Once Knew" shied away from the kinds of tonal resolution found in most pop songs, even songs by the Beatles. Yet it was a hit to some extent. One might argue that it would not have sold as well as it did if not sandwiched between monster Beach Boy hits of the time, riding the momentum. Still, it was a carefully crafted mixture of familiar voices and new ideas.

193

Brian is probably pleased with the "beautiful" introduction to this song because of what is missing (vocals) as much as what is present (instrumental music). I get the feeling at times that he would be happier creating instrumental rather than vocal statements, even though he is generally known for his vocal work. The introduction to "The Little Girl I Once Knew" is an example of artistic success resulting from the product being bigger than the sum of its parts. The parts include those non-harmonic, aggressive bass descents (bass fused with drum), those ascending and descending guitar phrases (minor and augmented intervals of the third and fourth), the rhythm triplets of the mixed-back organ, and the crucial tambourine. These elements of the introduction presage what is to come: the bass and vocal curve of the melody, the rhythm of the chorus. Like a proper overture, the introduction is itself a song.

> What sort of subliminal aural education was forcing itself upon me, at age 11, as I heard those strange chords, that jazzy bass line, those organ triplets?

Unlike any Beach Boys song that came before it, "The Little Girl I Once Knew" employs a doubled melody in which two vocal lines run together, combine, and coalesce. The result is very special — a sensed single melody which the listener swears he hears, yet which is not found on the charts. I believe that because of this series of interval syntheses in the opening melody, it is the most difficult Beach Boys melody to sing.

The opening lines, sung over a variety of G#minors, C#s, G#s, and more, offer no clue to the fact that the song is in the key of B. Then, after a satisfying rhythmic stop and two measures of complete silence, the chorus explodes with "She's not the little girl I once knew..."— now definitely in the key of B. Not to get too orthodox, however, Wilson modulates in the second choral phrase to a surprising D. The second verse attaches to the end of the chorus and is identical to the first verse musically except for an added final measure in which a cute bass figure leads into the second period of silence. The chorus explodes a second time.

Next comes a unique section, which is an elaboration of the chorus (around B and E). Four full measures of organ triplets evoke a shimmering joy, punctuated by a final burst of syncopated organ rhythm and

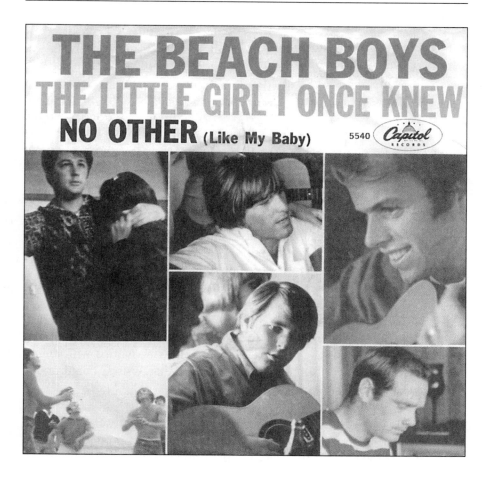

THE BEACH BOYS
THE LITTLE GIRL I ONCE KNEW
NO OTHER (Like My Baby)   5540 Capitol RECORDS

horns—the catharsis is complete. The alternation of B and E continues through six more measures in which the syncopated organ rhythm underscores some wonderful nonsense lyrics: "la doo day" and "pow pow pow"—the latter being used under the lyric of the returned chorus, which follows, now modulated to D. The chorus eases into a reprise of the instrumental introduction. The fade is the chorus in the root B. All told, the structure is something like IABABCDBI-fade.

The echoed rhythmic stops before the silences bear the stamp of Spector; Brian's falsetto in the circular chorus reaches back to the earliest Beach Boy songs; the organ throughout reminds one of the Wilson boys singing around a keyboard back in Hawthorne. The "dishing out" of vocal

> There is no evidence of the frail, sensitive man who would soon reach the limits of his musical and personal confidence and back down.

parts, including Love's "split man," also brings one back—to the philosophical construct that implied a group. Yet the complex song structure, the radical melody, the unorthodox chords, the inspired bass line, the silences, and fresh approaches to harmony and rhythm all speak of one artist at the leading edge of popular music in 1965.

A dangerous occupation of Brian Wilson watchers consists of trying to delineate periods or stages in his career. It is perhaps a worthless occupation. One finds so much overlapping of the years and ideas, that it would come as no surprise to learn he was thinking of *Smile* fragments in 1963. Even production techniques follow a foggy path upward through the years.

1965's "The Little Girl I Once Knew" stands with the contemporary "Sloop John B" and perhaps "Wouldn't It Be Nice" as highly sophisticated "Beach Boy songs." The ensuing *Pet Sounds* was filled with highly sophisticated "Brian Wilson songs." It appears that Wilson could create two types of music simultaneously.

The lyrics of "The Little Girl I Once Knew" were written by Wilson and mirror the extreme personal confidence that could produce the musical ideas in the song. He's talking about moving in on someone else's girl, joyously extolling her newfound maturity and virtue ("la doo day"). There is no evidence of the frail, sensitive man who would soon reach the limits of his musical and personal confidence and back down.

For reasons mentioned here and reasons that are difficult to put into words, "The Little Girl I Once Knew" stands alone. It is not quite like any other Brian Wilson song. While the songwriting, arranging, and production are avant-garde, the lyrics hearken to teenage concerns with a confidence of earlier works rather than the sensitivity of future works. That is a unique combination.

summer snapshot

By Don Cunningham

(Originally published in June 1980)

Now it is the summer of 1980. A radio contest promises that the winning entry of a "summer snapshot" will yield, for the photographer, a prize camera and publication on the next Beach Boys album. Which makes me wonder: Could current group manager Jerry Schilling become the Murry Wilson of the 1980s? And can he properly encourage Brian Wilson?

Coming out of the 1970s, with its surplus of successful hype (e.g., Village People) and minimum of musical integrity, one might ask whether the Beach Boys could become prey to the siren of artistic minimalism. Even they can get tired. Might they settle into a zone in which they are led by patent ideas rather than the creative vision of Brian Wilson?

At a recent concert Brian Wilson sat at the piano during the "gotta keep..." section of "Good Vibrations" and rolled his head around and around above the plane of his shoulders a good twenty times (try it). During "Surfer Girl" he played piano and sang while a plastic highway cone sat atop his head. He introduced "Rock And Roll Music" as "a slow ballad."

Whatever you make of those signs, Brian Wilson is functioning. In his own way. Here's hoping that in the years to come the fruits of the mystery that is Brian Wilson do not get swept under the rug as the band's promoters and image guardians make their decisions. In the Capitol years, Wilson was able to create great music despite sizable promotional demands and conceptual expectations. If the Beach Boys' future comes to reside in a womb of promotional concepts, will another *Pet Sounds* be possible? Let's hope for the best.